# GRACE
## moments

APRIL—JUNE 2022

Published by Straight Talk Books
P.O. Box 301, Milwaukee, WI 53201
800.661.3311 • timeofgrace.org

Copyright © 2022 Time of Grace Ministry

All rights reserved. This publication may not be copied, photocopied, reproduced, translated, or converted to any electronic or machine-readable form in whole or in part, except for brief quotations, without prior written approval from Time of Grace Ministry

Unless otherwise indicated, Scripture is taken from THE HOLY BIBLE, NEW INTERNATIONAL VERSION®. NIV®. Copyright © 1973, 1978, 1984, 2011 by Biblica, Inc.® Used by permission. All rights reserved worldwide.

Scripture marked EHV is from the Holy Bible, Evangelical Heritage Version® (EHV®) © 2019 Wartburg Project, Inc. All rights reserved. Used by permission.

Scripture marked ESV is taken from The Holy Bible, English Standard Version. Copyright © 2001 by Crossway Bibles, a publishing ministry of Good News Publishers.

Scripture marked GW is taken from GOD'S WORD®, © 1995 God's Word to the Nations. Used by permission of God's Word Mission Society.

Scripture marked KJV is taken from the King James Version. Text is public domain.

Printed in the United States of America
ISBN: 978-1-949488-56-2

TIME OF GRACE *is a registered mark of Time of Grace Ministry.*

# APRIL

Clap your hands, all you nations;
shout to God with cries of joy.

PSALM 47:1

**April 1**

# Seek truth
## Pastor Mike Novotny

It's hard to know what to do when you don't know what is true. I felt that way when COVID first hit. As the globe was scrambling to figure out what COVID was and how it worked, I laced up my shoes for some needed exercise. But as I trotted down my usual path, coming straight toward me was . . . a human! What should I do? Hold my breath as I run past her? Stand on a stranger's lawn so she can walk past with a six-foot buffer? I wasn't sure because it's hard to know what to do when you don't know what is true.

The same thing applies when your friend feels an attraction to her same sex. Or when one YouTube video tells you to pray the rosary and another tells you the rosary is wrong. Or when you're trying to find a good church, but the churches in town don't say the same thing. It's hard to know what to do when you don't know what is true.

Jesus once prayed to his Father, **"Your word is truth"** (John 17:17). In a world of feelings, emotions, opinions, traditions, partisan spins, man-made traditions, incomplete data, and conflicting sources, Jesus knew where to find a solid source of truth—the Word of his Father.

Few things in life matter more than making the time to seek the truth passionately through a dedicated study of God's Word. Because once God helps you figure out what is true, you'll know exactly what to do.

**April 2**

# My truth? Maybe!
Pastor Mike Novotny

Have you heard phrases like "be true to yourself," "live your truth," or simply, "my truth"? They seem to be the most popular doctrine of modern culture, appearing as the moral of most stories we find online. What would God say to that? Would he agree that you should look within to find truth?

Maybe. In speaking of the Gentiles who lacked the Scriptures, the apostle Paul once wrote, **"The requirements of the law are written on their hearts, their consciences also bearing witness, and their thoughts sometimes accusing them and at other times even defending them"** (Romans 2:15). Notice where God's law/truth was found—Their *hearts*. Their *consciences*. Their *thoughts*. All three of which are *within*.

Christian, if you are a Bible lover like me, you might instinctively recoil at the idea of "my truth." My first reaction is to push back, pointing out the selfishness that exists in the human heart that is all too willing to twist the truth to get its way. But perhaps we should first listen, searching for common ground, finding every spot where the conscience is correct.

If we believe the Bible is the truth (John 17:17), then let's believe that this verse is true too. That first step might lead to a conversation about the Word, where the whole truth can be found.

April 3

## My truth? Maybe not . . .
Pastor Mike Novotny

I have a love/hate relationship with my heart. I love it because, by God's grace, it has a lot of Scripture stored up in it. After years of church services, home devotions, and sermon podcasts, you can squeeze my heart and Bible will come beating out of it. The Holy Spirit has helped me treasure up God's Word and ponder it in my heart.

But I also hate my heart. Despite the services and sermons, I have noticed that when my heart feels cornered or criticized, it suffers from scriptural amnesia. It forgets everything that is good and true and of God. Instead, my heart goes into defensive mode, proudly pumping words toward my lips and producing detailed spreadsheets of all the things I do right and all the things my critics do wrong. That sin is part of my nature.

You too? The apostle Paul knew why following your heart or being true to yourself wouldn't lead you to the God-honest truth. He wrote, **"You must no longer live as the Gentiles do, in the futility of their thinking. They are darkened in their understanding and separated from the life of God because of the ignorance that is in them due to the hardening of their hearts"** (Ephesians 4:17,18). Notice the source of the problem—"In them."

The humbling reality is that our hearts cannot be completely trusted. So listen to your heart, but never let it get the final vote. Always bring it back to the Word, the only certain source of truth.

**April 4**

# Your truth = The truth?
Pastor Mike Novotny

The other day I studied every appearance of the word *truth* in the Bible. In my English translation, the word showed up 137 separate times. The question I wanted to answer, however, was how often *truth* was defined as "the truth" and how often it was described as "my/your truth." In other words, how did the inspired writers of the Bible think about the concept of truth?

The results were fascinating. Out of the 137 uses of *truth*, 99 of them had the word *the* before them. "The truth" was the most common way, by far, for the Bible to talk about the concept. What about "my truth"? From Genesis 1:1 to Revelation 22:21, that phrase showed up . . . 0 times. Never. Not once.

What about "your truth"? That combination actually did show up three separate times, which might lead some to think that truth could be subjective and personal. However, all three of those times were when the Bible's authors were speaking directly to God himself! In other words, those three "your truth's" were actually another way of saying "the truth."

The point of this research is that the Holy Spirit wants you to have a sure and certain source of truth. He never wants you to guess about good and evil or wonder about what's right and what's wrong. When it comes to God, especially his love for you and grace toward you, he wants you to know the truth. This is why Jesus prayed, **"Sanctify them by the truth; your word is truth"** (John 17:17).

**April 5**

## The gift of now
Christine Wentzel

Listening to the news and the watercooler gossip about the news, there's a pretty good consensus that everyone's positive everything's bad in the world. Trying to find any goodness and mercy in these stories is like searching for the proverbial needle in a haystack mixed with cow manure. Spend too long in the mire, and you're going to need a bath.

Allowing ourselves to take in this constant conscious or subconscious drip, drip, drip of negative messages undermines the daily work of the Holy Spirit. And this actually grieves the Holy Spirit. Before we know it, we're preoccupied by the past "should haves" or fearful of the future "what ifs." When we're distracted like this, it makes it more difficult to receive and make use of the God-given gifts that enliven and enable us to live a life pleasing to him—full of meaningful purpose, peaceful contentment, and joyful thanksgiving.

Let's accept today as a gift for what it is, a time of God's grace. Remain steadfast in this faith walk so that by it others may witness and seek out the Good News of salvation, now more than ever!

**"You know that when you were unbelievers, every time you were led to worship false gods you were worshiping gods who couldn't even speak. So I want you to know that no one speaking by God's Spirit says, 'Jesus is cursed.' No one can say, 'Jesus is Lord,' except by the Holy Spirit"** (1 Corinthians 12:2,3 GW).

**April 6**

# Left on read
Linda Buxa

For today's high school and college students, the worst thing you can do is leave them "on read." Let's pause a moment for a quick lesson because I'm guessing a number of you have no idea what this means. When you text, Snapchat, or DM someone, you can see if they have opened and read your message. If they don't answer quickly—or at all—you are left "on read." This is especially devastating when it comes to young romantic relationships. Leaving someone on read tells them you aren't actually interested in them.

It may sound silly to you when it comes to electronic communication, but you do know the great hurt that comes from feeling like you weren't being heard or answered—especially when it comes to God and your prayers. What if you've been praying and praying and he isn't answering the way you want him to? Maybe you feel like he's ignoring you. Perhaps you wonder if he is really invested in you.

God promises that, instead of worrying, you can rest assured that **"this is the confidence we have in approaching God: that if we ask anything according to his will, he hears us"** (1 John 5:14).

He listens. He hears. He acts.

P.S. To be fair, he doesn't always answer your prayers the way you think he should—and that's the hard part about being mature when it comes to faith. God does hear you, and he does respond, but sometimes what is for your best and for his glory isn't the answer you were praying for.

April 7

# You are normal
## Pastor Mike Novotny

When you find yourself addicted to destructive behavior, you might assume that you are not normal, the only one who struggles so deeply, so regularly, so pathetically.

But you'd be wrong.

The apostle Paul can relate to you: **"I do not understand what I do. For what I want to do I do not do, but what I hate I do. And if I do what I do not want to do, I agree that the law is good. As it is, it is no longer I myself who do it, but it is sin living in me. For I know that good itself does not dwell in me, that is, in my sinful nature. For I have the desire to do what is good, but I cannot carry it out. For I do not do the good I want to do, but the evil I do not want to do—this I keep on doing"** (Romans 7:15-19).

The human struggle versus the sinful nature might vary in its specifics (you lust, she worries, he gets angry), but we all have this in common—we don't do what we want. Not yet.

This truth is what drives us back to Jesus, trusting that only he can make us good enough to stand before the Father. And it drives us to each other, trusting that fellow Christians get it and would love to pray about it (James 5:16).

So don't let the devil convince you that you are too abnormal to belong. You belong here, in God's family, at the foot of the cross.

**April 8**

# The most important of all
Pastor David Scharf

Name some of the most important people and positions in our world. What did you come up with? Maybe you said, "The president, corporate CEOs, pro athletes, famous actors." Did you even think of a baptized child who lives for Jesus by helping others? Did you consider as most important a Christian mother who does the dishes or a Christian father who changes a diaper? What about an employee who tries to make his boss' company the best it can be? Did you think of yourself?

Jesus did. Jesus thought of you as he left the glory of heaven, where he received his due praise as King of kings and Lord of lords, to become your servant, to become human. Jesus valued you enough to serve you by living the perfect life of service God requires and then dying on a cross for all our service failures. Now Jesus thinks of you as "great" whenever you use your gifts to serve others. And it does not need to be feats of philanthropic proportions but the everyday opportunities that Jesus gives you as a parent, child, friend, coworker, etc.

Jesus said, **"Whoever wants to become great among you must be your servant"** (Matthew 20:26). The world has it all backward when identifying the most important people and positions. But you know what Jesus considers most important! God bless you today as you carry out your work of serving—the most important work of all!

April 9

# The day a tree stops growing
## Pastor Daron Lindemann

One of the largest and longest-living trees in the United States is the Seven Sisters Live Oak in Mandeville, Louisiana. This massive tree is estimated to be over one thousand years old.

And it's still growing!

Actually, there is no such thing as a full-grown tree. The day a tree stops growing, it dies. There is no such thing as a full-grown Christian or a full-grown church either.

We don't graduate from learning more about life and God and this world. We don't graduate from loving God and others more thoughtfully with resources we never knew we could employ. As a church we don't graduate once we've reached a certain size.

We don't graduate. We grow personally and organizationally. We keep growing, like a tree, reaching deep, wide, and high.

**"Physical training is of some value, but godliness has value for all things, holding promise for both the present life and the life to come. Be diligent in these matters; give yourself wholly to them, so that everyone may see your progress"** (1 Timothy 4:8,15).

We must not use the free gift of salvation as an excuse, because it is everything but. We are *not* required to grow in order to be saved, but when we are saved, then we are required to grow.

It's still grace. It's still a gift. Grow in godliness. Give yourself wholly.

April 10

# Which is better?
Pastor Clark Schultz

Which is better? Coke or Pepsi? LeBron or Jordan? Dairy Queen or Culvers? Okay, that last one is a trick question because all ice cream or custard is the best. These debates happen at the lunch table, watercooler, or even on the playground. We compare ourselves to others, and we do one of two things. We look down on the car they drive because ours is better, or we drive the minivan with the window sticker that reads, "I used to be cool."

Which side of the coin are you on? Do you look down on others, or do you use social media to look at what others have and think you've been ripped off in life?

Jesus' disciples had the "who is better" debate too. Imagine this conversation:

"Hey, Andrew!"

"Yeah, Peter."

"Remember that time we saw Jesus transfigured?"

"No, Peter. I don't."

"Oh yeah; that's right. You were at the bottom of the mountain. Stinks to be you brother!"

Jesus reminded his disciples and us that true greatness is not found in status or keeping up with the Joneses. Instead he said, **"Anyone who wants to be first must be the very last, and the servant of all"** (Mark 9:35). Jesus demonstrated this by showing the ultimate act of service and humility by living and dying for us all.

In a society of "me," Jesus' words are the best advice to follow.

**April 11**

# It's just a thing
Pastor Jon Enter

Do you know what happened to the first light bulb ever invented? After hundreds of hours of working by Thomas Edison, his errand boy dropped and shattered it. Edison went back to work making another. When it was completed, he gave the second light bulb to the same boy. Edison forgave that boy, showing him visible forgiveness.

If a loved one is in a horrible car accident but walks away unharmed, what often is the response? "I don't care about the car; I'm relieved you're okay." But if that same person backed up the car into a light pole, severely denting the bumper, what often is the response? Frustration. Anger. Yelling about how irresponsible the driver was.

Who carelessly damaged or destroyed something you care about? Did they apologize? Did you forgive them or make them feel terrible? Paul encourages us that no matter what someone does, **"you ought to forgive and comfort him, so that he will not be overwhelmed by excessive sorrow"** (2 Corinthians 2:7).

That's exactly what Thomas Edison did. That's exactly what Jesus does for you. That's exactly what Jesus wants from you. A dented car is just a thing. A new smartphone with a shattered screen is just a thing. A lost piece of jewelry is just a thing. We should be careful with the things God has given us, but things should not be more precious than pouring out forgiveness. Whom do you need to show visible forgiveness to?

**April 12**

# Self-control is a "fruit"
Pastor Mike Novotny

I wish self-control was a microwavable meal. Pop in a prayer request, wait a minute or two, and your self-control comes out, steaming and ready to resist sin.

But Paul didn't call self-control a microwavable meal. He called it "fruit." **"But the fruit of the Spirit is love, joy, peace, forbearance, kindness, goodness, faithfulness, gentleness and self-control"** (Galatians 5:22,23). The Holy Spirit can give you the strength to control yourself, even in a world where sin is always one second away, but he will produce that strength in you just like produce is produced.

First, you plant a seed of truth (grudge bearing or anger or drunkenness is bad; I am a holy child of God; I don't want to do this). Then, you water it with prayer (your prayers; the prayers of your closest allies). Next, you immerse that seed in the warm promises of God's love (during home devotions, while at church, through your worship playlist). And then, in due time, self-control shows up.

Forget about "fruit" and you'll get frustrated that you're not sin-free after a few weeks. Remember that this is "fruit" and you'll keep nourishing that seed until you become the kind of person you weren't before.

A person who enjoys the fruit of self-control.

**April 13**

# Keep confessing
## Pastor Mike Novotny

There is only one thing more agonizing than confessing your more embarrassing sins to another Christian. That *one thing* is confessing your embarrassing sins to another Christian *again*.

Here's why I say that—It takes tremendous courage to confess to a friend. However, after your confession happens, the temptation isn't over. Sometimes the tempter triples his efforts the very night that you brought your struggle into the light. And sadly, sometimes that temptation works. You fall. You fail. You take two steps back hours after that one bold step forward.

What do you say to your friend in that moment? How mortifying is it when that conversation didn't "work," not even for a week, perhaps not even for a day? The embarrassment is enough to make you avoid the issue altogether, to vaguely claim, "I'm doing pretty well this week . . ."

Please don't. When James wrote his classic verse on confession, his original Greek said, **"Keep confessing your sins to each other"** (James 5:16). The God who inspired his words knew that confession isn't a one-and-done sort of thing. It's a lifestyle, a habit, like going to the gym week after week, trusting that the repetition will produce real results.

So keep confessing. Whether it was a good week or a bad one, keep this part of your life in the light. This practice will give your inner circle another chance to encourage you, pray for you, and tell you the best news in the universe—Through Jesus you are already perfect.

**April 14**

## An opened mind
Christine Wentzel

While reading a study book on the 23$^{rd}$ Psalm, I was dangerously close to sleepwalking through the entire book. The author's study questions and answers were such familiar territory until I came to the author's chapter on the fourth verse. There her insight caused this sleepy-eyed student to stub her toes against a chest of treasure.

**"Even though I walk through the valley of the shadow of death, I will fear no evil, for you are with me"** (EHV). After I read through the verse, the author instructed me to go back and intentionally take note of the words *walk*, *through*, and *shadow*. She pointed out that I am not running in fear, not standing in terror, and not lost in the dark. Where there is shadow, there is light, and the Light in this valley is Christ, and he is with me!

The author of the study used a widely known portion of the Bible to highlight the faith-building treasures laying there for all to see. How many times do I miss the wealth of godly knowledge because I read and do not see?! The Lord's Spirit opened my mind to receive this treasure at the perfect time and also reminded me that his Word will accomplish his purpose. God's Word is alive, powerful, and true.

**"If you search for it like silver, if you hunt for it like hidden treasure, then you will understand the fear of the Lord, then you will find the knowledge of God, because the Lord gives wisdom"** (Proverbs 2:4-6 EHV).

**April 15** | Good Friday

## Never thirsty again
Pastor Clark Schultz

The thirstiest I've ever been was during my freshman year football practices. Our coaches would run us hard, and then the most glorious words were spoken: "Go get water." I remember running to the hose and sticking my whole head and face in the stream.

That, of course, is nothing compared to what our Lord experienced on the cross. One of the worst side effects of being nailed to a cross was raging thirst. Think of the emotional and spiritual struggle that increased his raging thirst. Judas betrayed him. His disciples deserted him. His countrymen condemned him. His own Father forsook him. Jesus was all alone on that cross, bearing the weight of the world's guilt. As the apostle Peter said, **"'He himself bore our sins' in his body on the cross"** (1 Peter 2:24). Jesus did this for us. His reason for doing this—YOU.

You are not a nameless, faceless number to our Lord. The One who knows the number of hairs on your head went to the cross for *you*. He endured the shame, the suffering, the curse, and even the thirst for *you*. And in so doing, he won complete forgiveness and eternal life for you.

In Revelation, John describes the saints in heaven with these words: **"'Never again will they hunger; never again will they thirst. . . . For the Lamb at the center of the throne will be their shepherd; 'he will lead them to springs of living water.' 'And God will wipe away every tear from their eyes'"** (7:16,17). We will enjoy that tear-free, thirst-free place, that place of living water, because the Lamb endured the thirst of crucifixion for us.

**April 16**

# Truth lasts forever
Pastor David Scharf

There is a legend told about a feast thrown by King Darius of Persia (the Daniel and the lions' den king). He gathered 127 governors from India to Ethiopia for a huge celebration. Part of the festivities was a contest among four young wise men who were to describe in one sentence the strongest thing in the world. Each wrote his sentence and submitted it. The first one said that wine is the strongest. The second, the king; the third, women; and the fourth, truth. The fourth wise youth explained his reason like this: "Wine, the king, and women are strong, but they are also wicked, and they perish. But truth endures forever. It is the strength, kingdom, power, and majesty of all ages."

As Christians, we couldn't agree more. Jesus said, **"When the Advocate comes, whom I will send to you from the Father—the Spirit of truth who goes out from the Father—he will testify about me"** (John 15:26). Jesus kept his promise to send the Spirit of truth at Pentecost. And what is the Holy Spirit's favorite topic? Jesus said, "He will testify about me." Just as on Pentecost when the disciples proclaimed the gospel in languages they did not know, so the Holy Spirit has been speaking truth in every language. And that truth has never changed. **"For God so loved the world that he gave his one and only Son"** (John 3:16). That truth lasts forever!

**April 17** | Easter Sunday

## New life
Andrea Delwiche

In the days preceding his death, Jesus reminded his disciples of a lesson from nature that had application in his own life and the lives of his followers.

**"Unless a kernel of wheat falls to the ground and dies, it remains only a single seed. But if it dies, it produces many seeds. Anyone who loves their life will lose it, while anyone who hates their life in this world will keep it for eternal life"** (John 12:24,25).

Jesus' followers were contemplating dreams of earthly glory. Jesus pointed them in a different direction. A kernel of wheat is only one seed until it falls to the ground and lies dormant for a season. Then in spring the soil warms; the seed germinates and grows. Later in its growth cycle, it bears fruit. The single kernel produces many kernels, which in turn will die, come back to life, and increase.

Through the giving of his own life, Jesus gave new life to his first-century disciples and to all of us who follow him today. We are in turn asked by God to give up our own lives for others.

Christ's resurrection resonates for us each day—both eternally and in time as we walk each day into the resurrection fields of loving service with Christ, our Savior and Redeemer. We love and serve others because Jesus loved and served us first. What an honor to be Christ-like in this way!

Christ is risen. Praise God! He is risen, and we rise with him. Hallelujah!

**April 18**

# Easter earthquake
## Pastor Daron Lindemann

Some of the worst earthquakes in our world's history have killed 200,000-300,000 people in each incident. The Bible says there was an earthquake when Jesus died, and then another earthquake when he rose to life.

**"There was a violent earthquake, for an angel of the Lord came down from heaven and, going to the tomb, rolled back the stone and sat on it"** (Matthew 28:2).

The earth's job is to hold people up (standing firmly) when we're alive and then to hold us in (buried and decomposing) when we're dead. However, it was forced to do the opposite to Jesus.

Roman soldiers sunk the bottom of a cross into the ground and crucified Jesus on it. The earth was holding Jesus up when he was dead. It convulsed at this moment. The innocent Son of God died!?

Jesus was buried in a tomb on Friday, and he came to life on Sunday. At that moment the earth was holding Jesus in when he was alive. It convulsed again. The living Son of God buried alive!?

These were the best earthquakes in our world's history. These moments saved millions and millions of people because Jesus did the miraculous, the unearthly, the otherworldly. He accomplished what normal and natural moments cannot.

The Bible says that Baptism connects believers to the death, burial, and resurrection of Jesus Christ (Romans 6:4). These moments save you from the natural instincts of sin and sinful pleasure, from physical limitations, and even death.

Earthshaking news!

**April 19**

## Spring = new life
Andrea Delwiche

"May God be gracious to us and bless us and make his face to shine on us—so that your ways may be known on earth, your salvation among all nations. May the peoples praise you, God; may all the peoples praise you. The land yields its harvest; God, our God, blesses us" (Psalm 67:1-3,6).

This psalm of thanksgiving and request for God's blessing reminds me, somewhat strangely, of Easter. The psalmist calls on God to renew the graciousness and favor that he has promised and demonstrated toward humanity since the beginning of time. And then the psalm celebrates a culmination: **"The land yields its harvest; God, our God, blesses us."**

The goodness of earthly harvest suggests pumpkins, apples, and the harvesting of crops in the fall. But the earth also yields its increase in spring—birds hatch, lambs are born on cold spring mornings, and seeds that have lain dormant all winter sprout and push their way through the cold earth.

For Christ followers, spring brings remembrance of our own new life. We were given a new beginning early one spring day more than two thousand years ago when Jesus returned to life, giving all humanity a spring beginning.

This new life, our spring, benefits us now. We won't reap the full harvest until we ourselves are raised from physical death, but as we live out our time of grace here on earth, we soak in God's love and live fruitful lives, blessed by God and blessing others.

Thanks be to God for his indescribable gift of love!

April 20

# Unzip that baggage
Pastor Clark Schultz

As a child of the 1980s, there were some interesting fashions: parachute pants, shoulder pads in sports coats, and my favorite—KangaRoos shoes, which were sneakers that had zipper pockets on each shoe. Why wouldn't you want zipper pockets on your feet?

While attending a big grade school basketball tournament, my mother gave me a roll of quarters to use for my food money. So Mr. Brainy here decided to shove all five dollars of quarters in both of his zipper shoe pockets. Never did it occur to my sixth-grade brain that I was walking around with a lot of extra weight. It also never dawned on me that while I played carrying all that currency in said shoes, that I was slower and couldn't move as quickly.

While diving for a ball, my shoe zippers burst open and quarters went rolling all over the wood gym floor. I can still see the officials tucking the quarters into their pockets and my coaches wondering, "Did he really have quarters in his shoes?"

**"You will again have compassion on us; you will tread our sins underfoot and hurl all our iniquities into the depths of the sea"** (Micah 7:19). What past sins are you lugging around? What keeps you awake at night with regret?

Friends, unzip the extra baggage and let it roll away. Christ reminds us that it is finished. Our sins are atoned for. You and I are free to hop around with joy—dare I say like kangaroos?!

April 21

# None.
## Pastor Mike Novotny

When I was studying New Testament Greek at Bible college, I can't say that I always loved it. Conjugating verbs and translating obscure words wasn't nearly as fun as playing FIFA on my Xbox.

But sometimes that effort brought back serious blessings. Like Romans 8:1. The English itself is glorious: **"Therefore, there is now no condemnation for those who are in Christ Jesus."** Just after admitting his constant struggle with sin in chapter 7, Paul declares that Christians like us are already saved through Jesus Christ.

But the Greek is even better. The Greek begins, "None, therefore . . ." Paul can't wait to tell us how much condemnation is left after the death and resurrection of Jesus—None! In English, we have to wait until the fifth word of the sentence ("*no* condemnation"), but Paul wanted the Romans to get the good news faster.

Isn't that amazing?! How much condemnation is hanging over your head right now? None. How much disapproval is left in God's eyes when he looks down on you? None. How many minutes do you need to worry about going to hell, falling from grace, or being rejected when heaven's feast begins? None.

If you are discouraged today, read how intensely Paul struggled in Romans 7:14-25. Then smile wide as he begins chapter 8 with a glorious word—

*None!*

**April 22**

# Jesus is worthy of the center spot
Pastor David Scharf

Is Jesus at the center of your life today? Or do you need to take care of many other things before you can get to him? In a Berlin art gallery, there once hung an unfinished picture by Adolph Menzel of Frederick the Great talking to his generals. There was a small bare patch in the center of the picture where a charcoal sketch indicated the artist's intentions. He had painted in all the generals, but he had left the king for last.

That seems lifelike to us, doesn't it? We carefully put in all the generals (work, family, house, car, etc.) and leave the King for last, with the hope that someday we may still get the King in the center. Menzel died before he could finish his picture. You can get to heaven without a house or family or riches, but you can't get there without Jesus.

The apostle Paul confessed, **"I consider everything a loss because of the surpassing worth of knowing Christ Jesus my Lord, for whose sake I have lost all things. I consider them garbage, that I may gain Christ"** (Philippians 3:8). Many dedicate their lives to gaining what Paul calls garbage and a loss. Is he going too far? Not at all. On your deathbed, nothing else matters except the knowledge of Jesus.

He is everything. The One who died that I might live is worth the center spot in my life and yours. Everything else pales in comparison!

**April 23**

## God's hands and feet
Andrea Delwiche

"Give the king your justice, O God, and your righteousness to the royal son! May he judge your people with righteousness, and your poor with justice! Let the mountains bear prosperity for the people, and the hills, in righteousness! May he defend the cause of the poor of the people, give deliverance to the children of the needy, and crush the oppressor!" (Psalm 72:1-4 ESV).

This psalm was written asking God's blessing for a king of Israel. We can incorporate these godly standards into our prayers for our own elected leaders.

We can also prayerfully consider our own "kingdoms," the places in our lives where we have authority and make decisions as citizens not only of our country but as citizens of the kingdom of heaven. How are we doing as being faithful stewards of the responsibilities God has given us?

Are we working for justice in our relationships? Are we defending the cause of the poor or giving deliverance to the children of the needy? Do we work to combat systems that oppress other people? Are our neighbors, no matter their ethnicity, preferences, or theology, precious in our sight?

*We* are God's hands and feet in this world. While God can act supernaturally to bring about change, mostly he chooses to work with you and me, giving us the privilege of loving and defending others. Ask the Holy Spirit to give you insight into how you can be the heart, hands, and feet of Jesus in your community.

**April 24**

# You are not a black sheep
Pastor Mike Novotny

When Ananias reached out his hands toward the serial killer, I wonder if they were trembling. God had spoken directly to Ananias, sending him to the house where Saul of Tarsus was sitting, praying, and waiting.

Ananias knew what every believer in Damascus did, namely, that Saul was a bad man. He was obsessed, violent, and relentless, the kind of guy who would walk six marathons to travel from Jerusalem to Damascus to find a Christian, arrest a Christian, and kill anyone who dared to claim that Jesus was the Christ.

So when Ananias met that Saul, the Saul who came to kill him, what would he say? Acts 9 tells us, **"Then Ananias went to the house and entered it. Placing his hands on Saul, he said, 'Brother Saul'"** (verse 17).

No joke. The first word out of his lips was *brother*. "Saul, you are my brother in Christ. Saul, you are part of my Father's family too. Saul, despite what you have done, you belong at the table as my brother in faith."

If you have been struggling with sin, whether drinking too much or worrying too much or losing your cool too much, it's tempting to wonder which word Christians would use to describe you. *Weak? Self-destructive? Embarrassing?* But that is not who you are. In Christ you get a new name, purchased at the cross and guaranteed by the empty grave.

Through faith in Jesus, you are my brother or my sister, my sibling in the holiest family on earth. Believe it and live according to it.

**April 25**

# DEBT: A four-letter word
Pastor Jon Enter

Debt can make you do spiritually dumb things. Debt causes stress, affecting your relationships and your waistline. Debt causes fights over spending habits (some are savers; some are impulse buyers . . . which one are you?). Debt causes lying and deception. Debt causes unfaithfulness in offerings to God. Debt destroys.

Jesus came in humility, showing that the most valuable things aren't things. Jesus was born into a poor family, in a backwater town, to a conquered people. As an adult, Jesus had no place called home. He lived as a wanderer, couch surfing the countryside. Don't misunderstand. Jesus was no lazy leech. He chose not to focus on money but on making his Father pleased with his perfect living. He taught us to focus not on money but on our Maker.

**"It was not with perishable things such as silver or gold that you were redeemed . . . but with the precious blood of Christ"** (1 Peter 1:18,19). God has freed you, forgiven you, and released you from the devilish control that money desires to have over you. You were not saved with perishable things, so don't live to save up perishable things.

There are nearly 2,200 Bible passages dealing with money and materialism. How do you step free from its control? A.B.C.

Acknowledge all you have comes from God. Use it well.

Budget God's money. Use it well.

Control your spending. Use it well.

When you do, the stress of debt will stop pulling your focus off God. Control your money so your money doesn't control you.

**April 26**

# How many motives?
Pastor Mike Novotny

If I made you write an essay listing all the reasons to avoid sin, how long would your essay be?

I wouldn't give you a minimum word count or force you to cite your references in APA style (I'm not a monster!), but I wonder if you could find a pen and scribble down all the motivating reasons that pop into your mind. Fix your eyes on all the good things that God loves and that sin threatens, reminding your heart that our Father truly knows best. Go ahead. I'll wait.

To get you started, let me list my top two. Second on my list is the drama that sin causes in my life. King David wrote, **"Those who run after other gods will suffer more and more"** (Psalm 16:4). The false god of pleasure asks me to sacrifice too much—my integrity, my time, my honesty, my intimacy. The more sin I run after, the more I suffer.

But even more motivating than such loss is Jesus' love. **"For Christ's love compels us"** (2 Corinthians 5:14). The more we meditate on Jesus' love, the love that gave up all pleasure and endured such pain, the more we simply don't want to sin. We have found something more satisfying, more enjoyable, more interesting than sin could ever provide. We have found a love that never fails.

Reflect on those two reasons and add a few of your own. God motivates us in many ways to say no to sin and yes to him.

**April 27**

## Reassurance
Christine Wentzel

"For I am convinced that neither death nor life, neither angels nor demons, neither the present nor the future, nor any powers, nor height nor depth, nor anything else in all creation, will be able to separate us from the love of God that is in Christ Jesus our Lord" (Romans 8:38,39).

What blessed assurance that my Savior has my back! I picture Jesus looking over my head, holding all those deadly bullies at bay with one blazing, glorified stare. Praise the Lord!

Sadly, there are times I take this for granted by handling business on my own. When I'm at this too long, I'm tempted to drift away from consistent worship, study, and prayer until the next day, next week, next month, or, God forbid, the next year.

On my own, doubt creeps in when my broken-down, aging body no longer follows orders from my frustrated brain. My frustrated brain loses control of my disappointed heart. My disappointed heart demands justice according to my sense of fairness. Before long I'm tempted to become uncertain that my holy Champion is still there.

It's not just the outside enemies trying to steal me away; it's the enemy within as well. It's time to go back to Romans 8. By God's grace, Christ my King is still there. I look into his blazing eyes of compassion. I sink to my knees in repentance in the realization I allowed pride to usurp his sovereignty over this new life he gifted to me.

Nothing will separate me, not even myself, praise the Lord!

**April 28**

# Why, God?
## Pastor Clark Schultz

A friend, colleague, husband, and father is suddenly called home to heaven. Why, God? Bluntly speaking, life stinks. When we grieve, and trust me, we will, we go through the following steps: denial, anger, bargaining, and depression.

We deny that God could take our dad, child, or best friend. "No, you have to be kidding." Soon we realize there will be no more text messages between the two of you or a warm embrace. We become mad—mad at the world and at God. Why, God? This leads to thinking we have some control over the matter. "If I had just told him not to go on the snowmobiling trip, he'd still be here today." Or, "If I had done a better job at being a dad, I would have noticed the symptoms earlier." Wrong! When this proves hopeless, depression can set in. The devil works overtime during this period to get us to think God does not care.

Dear reader, where are you on this grief roller coaster? Grief and mourning are real. I have said this before, and I echo it again. It is okay to ask for help. Yes, of course, from your Father in heaven, but also professional help and help from others who have gone through this. Then the final stage of acceptance can take place and you can say with the psalmist: **"My times are in your hands; deliver me from the hands of my enemies, from those who pursue me"** (31:15).

**April 29**

# Dispel our doubts
Pastor David Scharf

Fill in the blank to describe this well-known Bible character: _____ Thomas. I bet you got it: Doubting Thomas. He wasn't there that first Easter Sunday evening when the risen Jesus appeared to the other disciples. Can you imagine the disciples saying to him, "Jesus really showed up! It was awesome!" Well, Thomas refused to believe it. A week later, Jesus appeared again. This time Thomas got to see him with his own eyes and touch him with his own hands. Jesus said, **"Reach out your hand and put it into my side. Stop doubting and believe"** (John 20:27). Thomas was no longer Doubting Thomas!

I had a friend in high school who always struggled with some challenge to what the Bible says. He would wrestle with it, and God would lead him to understand, but then another doubt would pop up. I thought, "Why does that happen to him?" A better question might be, "Why does that happen to us?" It has to do with our approach to what Jesus says. We don't believe it because we can prove it. We believe it because the powerful and risen Son of God says it. It's true. Living in that truth dispels our doubts! When we have doubts, where do we turn? Right back to our Savior who encourages, **"Blessed are those who have not seen and yet have believed"** (John 20:29).

April 30

## The truth
Pastor Clark Schultz

If I hold up three fingers and ask you, "How many fingers am I holding up?" I'm hoping you say three. It would be foolish to see the three fingers and say, "Nope. I don't believe you; you have four fingers up." Or what if I make the game even simpler and say, "I'm holding up three fingers," and you still insist I'm holding up four fingers? That would be a complete denial of what's in front of you—the truth. I know this is an odd analogy, but hear me out. There's a point; I promise.

Why is it when God tells us we are **"fearfully and wonderfully made"** (Psalm 139:14), instead of praising him like the rest of that verse says, we often insist it's not true? We look in the mirror and feel ashamed of what we see. We scroll on social media and compare ourselves to others—and we fall short in our minds. We take the lack of likes on our Facebook posts to mean we're failures. We think we have no purpose or no special gifts or talents to contribute anything to anyone.

Dear friend, believing these lies is like holding up three fingers and saying there are four. When you see three fingers held up, that's the truth . . . three fingers. The same is true about what God says about you. He made you—fearfully and wonderfully! He loves you—enough to send his only Son to save you! He gave you unique gifts and talents to be used to his glory—yes, he did! (See 1 Peter 4:10 or Romans 12:6-8.)

You can praise God with all of Psalm 139:14: **"I praise you because I am fearfully and wonderfully made; your works are wonderful, I know that full well."**

God doesn't make junk; that's the truth.

# MAY

"I am the vine; you are the branches.
If you remain in me and I in you,
you will bear much fruit;
apart from me you can do nothing."

JOHN 15:5

**May 1**

## Jesus woos, not woes
Pastor David Scharf

In one of Aesop's fables, the wind and sun prepared to make a man shed his coat. The wind used its violence and force to tear the coat off, but the man only bound himself all the more within it. The sun gradually used its warmth on the man, and he voluntarily shed the coat himself. In a way, the sun wooed him to want to take off his coat.

This is how Jesus wants to win you. Jesus said of the people of Israel, **"How often I have longed to gather your children together, as a hen gathers her chicks under her wings"** (Luke 13:34). Sadly, they were not willing. But here is the point. Jesus does not shame you with woes. He does not force or intimidate you. Instead, he longs to gather you by warming your heart with his love and reminding you of what he's done.

No matter how many times you and I try to scurry away from Jesus, he gathers us back under the wings of his forgiveness. How? He woos us with his words, *"Then neither do I condemn you . . . surely, I am with you always . . . in my Father's house are many rooms."* No matter how often we stray, Jesus woos us back by showing us just how much he loves us. Far more than any hen for her chicks. Jesus suffered hell on a cross so that you and I would go to heaven. Now we are safe under Jesus' wings!

**May 2**

## How's your journey going?
Andrea Delwiche

Some biblical scholars believe Psalm 71 was written by King David in the later years of his life to reflect upon the journey that he had taken with the Lord from conception onward. From these verses, we get an intimate sense of how David viewed his lifelong relationship with God:

**For you, O Lord, are my hope, my trust, O Lord, from my youth. Upon you I have leaned from before my birth. . . . So even to old age and gray hairs, O God, do not forsake me, until I proclaim your might to another generation, your power to all those to come"** (verses 5,6,18 ESV).

How would you chronicle your history with the Lord? Can you look back to childhood and see, especially with the benefit of years, how God taught you? Or do you remember a point in your teenage years or adulthood when you first realized that God was walking with you and guiding you?

Perhaps even now you are contemplating how to trust God and let him teach and guide and protect your every step. David's testimony gives us an example of what wholehearted faith looks like and sounds like. David's relationship with God was mature and well-tested.

How would you describe your journey? What if you sat down and wrote a psalm of praise to God for the work he has done in your life? Ask the Holy Spirit to guide you as you contemplate the journey that you've been taking with the Lord.

May 3

## Seek and save
### Linda Buxa

"**For the Son of Man came to seek and to save the lost**" (Luke 19:10).

In October 2021, a hiker was lost in Colorado. As part of their search, rescuers called the hiker's smartphone but never got ahold of her. You know why she didn't answer? Not because service was bad but because she didn't recognize the number! That's right. She was lost, but because she didn't know who was calling, she didn't answer the phone.

It's an amusing story because ultimately it turned out okay, but it made me think about people who are spiritually lost. Maybe, just like the lost hiker, they won't answer a spiritual rescue call from a stranger. When people are lost, they might not be open to talking about sin and grace, heaven and hell, with a stranger. Honestly, I don't blame them. Who wants to open up about such deeply personal things with someone who hasn't earned the right to have that conversation?

Ah, but when the same message comes from someone who knows them, loves them, and cares for them, it has a far bigger impact. They will be far more open to it when a friend says, "I was lost too, and Jesus came looking for me. Mind if I share my amazing story of being rescued?"

You know someone who is lost. Start by making the call. There may not be much time left.

**May 4**

## Pray for people
Pastor Mike Novotny

I hear a lot of confessions about pornography. Both men and women, young and old, married and single schedule a time to talk and, for the first time, bring their darkness into the light.

My response to these courageous confessions is almost always the same. First, I tell them God loves them. Second, I thank them for trusting me enough to talk about it. Third, I try to figure out how intense their struggle is. Fourth, I ask them a question: Whom in your life could you talk to about this?

For some, that question is easy to answer. But for others, it's met with silence. It's hard to know who would respond well to their sexual sin, whom they could trust, and who would want to help them fight for self-control.

How about you? Who in your life could you talk to about this sin (or any other)? If someone immediately comes to mind, praise God! Reach out today and keep confessing. But if you are unsure, here's where to start—pray for people. Pray that God would open your eyes to a person who is fully capable of walking with you, someone in your church or in your circle of friends, someone who would be honored to pray for you so you may be healed.

**"Ask and it will be given to you; seek and you will find; knock and the door will be opened to you. For everyone who asks receives; the one who seeks finds; and to the one who knocks, the door will be opened"** (Matthew 7:7,8).

**May 5**

## Stage presence
Christine Wentzel

Everyone has stage presence in the virtual world of social media. There we can create our own realities while interacting on a global scale like never before. It's in these digital settings we usually don't hesitate to tie ourselves up in knots like we might in face-to-face situations. We share our thoughts, actions, and whereabouts in the most excruciating, even hyperbolic, detail. False courage grows in this so-called safe setting.

Let's reevaluate our stage presence. Who is the star? Is it real? Who makes guest appearances? Do we text, tweet, pin, or email **"whatever is true, whatever is noble, whatever is right, whatever is pure, whatever is lovely, whatever is admirable"** (Philippians 4:8)?

Our fingertips are a tap away from posting and sharing some of the most uplifting Christian faith stories! Let's grab the opportunity to share how awesome the work of Jesus really is. Provide information that will send people seeking answers to their lives from Bible-believing ministries like Time of Grace. There they will discover Jesus in every platform available. Use the Word of God to speak power that enlivens dead souls for heaven's sake!

Whether our audience is a few or in the millions, there are lost souls in our circles who need to know a personally invested Lord and Savior is their Morning Star in this dark world. Let's step aside and announce Christ has the center stage.

**"Whatever you have learned or received or heard from me, or seen in me—put it into practice. And the God of peace will be with you"** (Philippians 4:9).

**May 6**

# Lipstick and a toilet brush
## Pastor Daron Lindemann

A high school principal was frustrated by the repeated lipstick graffiti on the girls' bathroom mirrors.

One day she asked a group of girls to assemble in the bathroom. She showed them the lipstick graffiti and explained how much extra work this was for the custodian.

Then she asked the custodian to dip a toilet brush in a toilet and clean the mirror with it. The girls didn't use their lipstick on the mirror again!

I would add one more thing. After the custodian cleaned off the lipstick with the toilet brush, I would have him shine up the mirror and make it dazzle. Then I would have each girl look in the mirror, and I'd ask, "Who do you see?"

I'd answer, before they could say a word: "A daughter of God." I'd teach that daughters of God are princesses in his kingdom—very precious, perfectly pure, desired by Jesus Christ himself.

The attention-getting graffiti and validation of peers isn't needed because the goodness of God and gifts of God are true.

**"Don't be deceived,"** the Bible says. **"Every good and perfect gift is from above, coming down from the Father of the heavenly lights, who does not change like shifting shadows"** (James 1:16,17).

What lies of the devil do you believe most often that cause you to seek filthy attention and sin? Don't be deceived. Live your true identity as a child of God. That identity is a good and perfect gift.

**May 7**

# Who does that?
Pastor David Scharf

"Who does that?" That question can be a wonderful compliment, like when you hear a story of someone donating their kidney to a total stranger. Or the question can be shocking disbelief in a negative way, like when someone shows unusual cruelty to another who didn't deserve it.

The Bible writers consistently look at God and ask, "Who does that?" Only it's never in the negative way. What do you do for people who are born enemies, whose lives give evidence of that inborn hatred, who walk away from you with their thoughts, words, and actions—who don't fully admit the sin in their lives?

God's answer? You die for them. You forgive them. It is what lead Micah the prophet to burst out, **"Who is a God like you, who pardons sin and forgives the transgression of the remnant of his inheritance? You do not stay angry forever but delight to show mercy"** (Micah 7:18). Think of how unlike anyone or anything our God is. Every other "god" of every world religion teaches salvation by good works. In order to please their gods, they must do good works. Adherents are forced to ask, "What must I do?" In Christianity, we do good works *because* God is already pleased. Christians instead ask, "What has God done?" We are compelled to look at Jesus' cross in awe with the Bible writers and ask, "Who does that? Who is a God like you who pardons sins?"

**May 8** | Mother's Day

## Moms, you are valuable to Jesus
Andrea Delwiche

**"Mary . . . sat at the Lord's feet listening to what he said. But Martha was distracted by all the preparations. . . . 'Martha, Martha,' the Lord answered, 'you are worried and upset about many things, but few things are needed—or indeed only one. Mary has chosen what is better, and it will not be taken away from her'"** (Luke 10:39-42).

Moms, this is not a devotion to tell you that you are worried over many things. Moms feel incredible pressure to provide for their families. But you are much more than your to-do list and the pressures of post-worthy pictures and idyllic family stories.

You are valuable to Jesus as a human being with a thirsty soul. You are *capable of* and *need to* sit at Jesus' feet and learn from him. Jesus deeply desires to sit and talk with you. He looks at you and says, "Sit with me. Let's talk, and you will learn from me." One sister sat at Jesus' feet, and Jesus *defended her* for doing it.

The time you spend with Jesus will be given back to you. God is so generous in this regard. Your priorities will shift and give you ease.

Only Jesus can fill our deepest longing. Let your mothering flow from that peace, free from self-criticism or criticism from others. You are one of Jesus' most valued followers.

**May 9**

## The uniqueness of Jesus
Pastor Mike Novotny

Decades ago, at a European conference, scholars discussed the world's religions, wondering if there was anything unique about the Christian faith. Was it prayer? No, almost every religion prays. An afterlife? No, most religions believe in some sort of heaven and/or hell. Doctrine? Too common. Commandments? Standard. Men in fancy hats? The norm.

But then, according to church legend, C. S. Lewis entered the room, the Oxford professor who had converted to Christianity in his early 30s. What's unique about the Christian faith? "That's easy," Lewis replied. "Grace."

That's true. The earliest followers of Jesus Christ were uniquely infatuated with grace. Study the loaded word *grace* in the New Testament and you'll learn that grace reaches people, appears to people, and is poured out on people so that they find grace, receive grace, believe by grace, and share in grace. Christians, the Scriptures say, are people chosen by grace, called by grace, saved by grace, justified by grace, living in grace, and living under grace. Grace is with us, works in us, and sufficient for us. Grace overflows, increases, reigns, strengthens, and gives access to God. That's why we set our hope on grace, grow in grace, and preach the glorious grace of God. In fact, the very last verse of the entire Bible says, **"The grace of the Lord Jesus be with God's people. Amen"** (Revelation 22:21).

Grace gets the last word because the Christian faith is about grace. Undeserved love. Surprising favor. I can't imagine believing any other way. Can you?

**May 10**

# Quiet; be still
## Pastor Jon Enter

I've never been in a boat in rough water. Have you? I almost drowned when I was about ten, so choppy water makes me anxious. I couldn't imagine how bad the storm must've been for the disciples for them to cry out to Jesus, **"Don't you care if we drown?"** (Mark 4:38).

What storm is pummeling your life, causing you to doubt God's power? No matter what you've done, no matter how hard you've tried to rise above, you sink further into despair that your situation is hopeless. The pounding of the waves of worry are relentless when the storm surrounds you. It's easy to be overwhelmed.

For the disciples, Jesus was physically right there, but they doubted his concern for their lives. What's amazing is how Jesus responded to their accusation: **"He got up, rebuked the wind and said to the waves, 'Quiet! Be still!'"** (Mark 4:39). Notice that Jesus didn't rebuke the water; he told the water to be still. Jesus rebuked the wind that caused the chaos. When the wind's power over the water was removed, the water was calm.

When you struggle to see God's power and even when you come to him unsure of how he will intervene, you still come to him. You know he is the only way peace can come, even if you don't understand how. Jesus will rebuke and remove the sin and uncertainty overtaking your life. When it's gone, quietness and calm will come.

**May 11**

# You shine!
Pastor Daron Lindemann

In the rural hill country of Texas, miles away from city lights, many more stars appear in the night sky. It puts my constellation skills to the test. Where exactly is the North Star?

If you can locate the outer edge of the Big Dipper's bowl (the edge farther from the handle), draw an imaginary line extending from the star on the bottom through the star on the top. This line takes you directly to the North Star.

It takes a bit of knowledge and practice—or an app on your phone—to identify constellations. But there is one star you have no problem identifying. The sun! Same with the moon at night. Much more obvious.

You probably even know how the moon shines light. The moon doesn't generate its own light, like the sun, but reflects the light of the sun.

The Bible says that Christians are **"children of light"** (Ephesians 5:8). We don't generate our own light, like children don't bring themselves into existence. We reflect a greater light. The light of God.

God shines. Believe in him, and you are enlightened by him, like the moon. You shine too. Others can look at you and say, "I see a reflection of God." No, you aren't God. Just like the moon is not the sun. But you do shine with God's light.

The Bible calls both Jesus and his believers **"the light of the world"** (John 8:12; Matthew 5:14). So go shine today!

**May 12**

# The cure
## Christine Wentzel

I am one of over 14 million people who suffer from some form of autoimmune disease. If you add those who suffer from the thousands of other diseases and disorders, there are few left untouched by chronic illness.

However, there's one fatal disease we all have in common—it's called sin. Even the healthiest, most self-aware people innately know something is not right inside of them thanks to their natural knowledge of God. Every person experiences variations of hate, sadness, conflict, intolerance, meanness, illness, disregard, brutality, and overindulgence, and all of it ends in death. We adopt various lifestyles, choose the latest health fads, chase down scientific studies, and enact societal laws to pursue a paradise lost on the earth.

**"Nevertheless, I will bring health and healing to it; I will heal my people and will let them enjoy abundant peace and security"** (Jeremiah 33:6).

Out of compassionate love, God promised to send the cure to us while we were still sinning against him. His Son, Jesus, willingly laid aside his immortality for a mortal life lived in perfect obedience for us. He fulfilled all the Old Testament prophecies predicting his coming rescue for humankind. He took the sin of all humanity upon himself. He destroyed the power of the grave by walking out of his.

Our hope for all that is broken and dying is found in only one cure, Christ Jesus. May we triage people's sickness of sin with his Spirit-driven, love-joy-peace-patience-kindness-goodness-faithfulness-gentleness-self-control Good News medicine!

**May 13**

# Guardrails
Pastor Mike Novotny

Over a decade ago, I heard a brilliant teaching on the need for adding rules to the Bible.

If that sounds bad, it wasn't. It was wise. The pastor talked about personal "guardrails," rules that keep us far from the edge of a tragic fall into sin. For example, if you struggle with drunkenness, limiting yourself to one drink (or no drinks!) might be a guardrail that keeps you from going over the edge and hurting the people whom God loves so dearly. There is no passage that demands, "You shall have no more than one drink," but there is wisdom in knowing yourself and acting accordingly.

**"Be very careful, then, how you live—not as unwise but as wise"** (Ephesians 5:15).

What would a wise guardrail look like in your life? If anger is your issue, which triggers could you avoid that too often lead to your outbursts? Is it watching certain channels or visiting certain websites? If so, have the wisdom to cut temptation off before temptation even arrives.

You will never regret looking back and playing it safe with your holiness. So be a student of your own story, note the times/places/situations that are most often connected to your sin, and make the bold choice to stay far from the cliff of temptation.

That's how wise people live.

**May 14**

# What's your secret?
## Pastor Jon Enter

Hello. My name is Jon Enter. Husband. Father of four. Pastor. Coach. Sin addict.

And so are you. You may not see it. You may not be willing to admit it. But you are. You have sins you know are wrong, but you do them anyway. You want to stop. You can't or, really, you won't stop. You're an addict. And so am I. You can't keep your dirty little obsession a secret forever.

Just ask the family of Diane Schuler. In 2009 she hid her alcohol addiction from her family. She drove intoxicated into oncoming traffic resulting in her own death and the deaths of seven innocent people. Then her family and the nation learned the truth.

What is it?

What's your addiction? The devil is unoriginal. He uses the same tired temptations against you. Why? It works. It works so well because the excuses flow freely. "I can stop at any time." "It's not that bad." "No one knows." "I'm in control." "It's not as bad as . . ."

Addiction makes you do irrational things, like making excuses over what you know is terribly hurting you physically, emotionally, and spiritually. It's hard to admit you're powerless to temptation that's trying to squeeze the life out of your soul. **"Humble yourselves before the Lord, and he will lift you up"** (James 4:10). God will lift you up because he lifted up his Son upon a cross to pay the price for you to free you from the clutches of the devil. Humble yourself. And you will be lifted up.

**May 15**

# God is with you
Pastor Clark Schultz

It was mid-July. A discussion broke out in our car between our two older boys regarding when school was going to start.

"Not soon enough," mumbled the parents under their breath (☺). But being the adults, we told our middle child that school would be starting in less than a month. His five-year-old response cracked us up: "A whole month? That's like a whole week away!"

**"But do not forget this one thing, dear friends: With the Lord a day is like a thousand years, and a thousand years are like a day"** (2 Peter 3:8). Is this saying our God is on toddler time? I mean, think about it. When you were younger, summers seemed to last forever, but then you grew up and thought, "Where did the time go? It seems the days are speeding by." There are days when you feel like you're trapped in the eternal car ride of sickness, bills, and fights with siblings. Those days don't seem to speed by quickly enough.

We live in a broken world. Sin makes the miserable times seem like eternity and the good times like catching water in our hands. In both cases, God is God. His timetable is not ours, and he is not bound by the minutes and seconds we hold so dear. While this can seem frightening, remember Hebrews 13:8: **"Jesus Christ is the same yesterday and today and forever."**

Months, weeks, yesterday, today, and tomorrow you are with God.

**May 16**

# How much does Jesus love you?
## Pastor Daron Lindemann

I need to choose from my many shoes and shirts which to wear each day. As a matter of fact, I have to choose which closet I go to. When I'm hungry, I stand in front of the fridge, not for lack of food but because the options take time to consider.

How much does Jesus give to you? How much healing and hope? How much mercy? How much provision and power? How much of his personal presence?

When he suffered and died for you, did he throw his hands in the air and say, "Enough! I can't take anymore" and bail out? How attentive is he when listening to your prayers? Does he watch the birds flit around for entertainment while you are droning on and on about your troubles?

How much does Jesus love you? More than you need.

**"I have come that they may have life, and have it to the full"** (John 10:10).

Jesus miraculously fed over five thousand hungry people so full that his disciples collected leftover food. He fills your life with more than you need. Follow him and you'll find more than morsels.

Jesus miraculously turned water into not just any wine but the best of the best wine. He abundantly turns your empty hopes and dreams into the best of his best blessings. Drink from him and you'll be filled.

Jesus gives you more than necessary, more than you need, more than enough. Be satisfied with him more than everything else.

**May 17**

## A conversation with God
### Andrea Delwiche

Here's an honest conversation with God:

"**When my soul was embittered, when I was pricked in heart, I was brutish and ignorant; I was like a beast toward you. Nevertheless, I am continually with you; you hold my right hand. You guide me with your counsel, and afterward you will receive me to glory. Whom have I in heaven but you? And there is nothing on earth that I desire besides you. My flesh and my heart may fail, but God is the strength of my heart and my portion forever**" (Psalm 73:21-25 ESV).

It seems the psalm writer had been harboring bitterness toward God. We get an intimate look at his thought process—first the grievance and then a slowly developing realization that opens like a rosebud. This psalm becomes a heartfelt cry of love for God.

These words could be an entry point into a deeper relationship with God for us. Sometimes we are opposed to God. Our hearts feel like blocks of wood. But beneath the emotions lie hope and longing for relationship with God.

It's good to have a conversation with God about disappointment and anger. He can handle it. The Holy Spirit may guide us into fuller understanding.

Yes, there is inequity, injustice, and brokenness. And yes, God is with us. We live and have our being in God's intimate company. The words of the psalmist are our own: "**I am continually with you; you hold my right hand. You guide me with your counsel, and afterward you will receive me to glory.**"

**May 18**

# Temporary residents
## Pastor Clark Schultz

While visiting Charleston recently, I heard the unique legend and mystery of former Vice President John C. Calhoun's grave. Calhoun was buried in Washington D.C. and then exhumed and moved to Charleston to a "strangers" grave—one for people who were not Charleston natives.

Then during the Civil War, his body was again exhumed and moved to an unmarked grave in a "friendly" graveyard as a precaution against any Union troop desecration. This graveyard was reserved for members of the congregation who were born in Charleston. According to legend, after the war Calhoun's body was moved back to its current sight—the "strangers" graveyard.

The Bible reminds us that we are **"aliens and temporary residents"** (1 Peter 2:11 EHV). Some Bible translations use the word *strangers*. There's even a popular hymn by Thomas R. Taylor that says, "I'm but a stranger here; heaven is my home."

For the believer, there will be no shuffling from grave to grave, just this: **"For the Lord himself will come down from heaven, with a loud command, with the voice of the archangel and with the trumpet call of God, and the dead in Christ will rise first"** (1 Thessalonians 4:16). The war is over. The battle is won. We are on the winning side, and Jesus himself says, **"I have called you friends"** (John 15:15).

My grave or yours, be confident that the only time we will be moved is when Jesus welcomes us home.

**May 19**

# Your activity is not your identity
Pastor Mike Novotny

Years ago I tapped into my Bible nerdery and tried to count all the names that Christians are called in the New Testament. In some verses, we are called "sinners," "weak," and "of little faith" while in other verses we are called "saints," "strong," and "loved" by the Lord.

For souls who are already perfect in Christ but not yet perfect in our behavior, this makes sense.

What shocked me, however, is the ratio of bad names to good names. If my unofficial tally is correct, I found 72 bad names (sinners, weak, etc.) in the New Testament and—you ready for this?—610 good names! 610! For every one time that God calls us "sinners," nine times he calls us "saints"!

I wonder if this is what Paul alluded to when he wrote, **"But where sin increased, grace increased all the more"** (Romans 5:20). Yes, our sins are many, but his grace is more. Much, much, much more.

So as you go through the daily battle to deny self and honor God with your life, feel free to call yourself a sinner. The Bible does. But if you want to be biblically balanced, then call yourself all the other names too—

Holy. Pure. Loved. Chosen. Justified. Sanctified. Redeemed. Blameless. Spotless.

That's not me trying to make you feel better about yourself. That's God reminding you of your incredible identity in Christ Jesus.

**May 20**

# Don't just get by
## Pastor Clark Schultz

A famous superhero claims that his shield is made from the strongest metal on earth. Nothing can break it! In Ephesians 6:16, the apostle Paul reminds us that we have something stronger: **"the shield of faith."**

The object of our faith is Jesus, and he is the strongest of all. How much are you connecting to him? A small amount of faith saves, middle-of-the-road faith saves, and all-hands-on-deck faith saves because of the object of that faith—Jesus.

But for those of us who look to "just get by," what happens when the wind and waves of debt, divorce, or depression come crashing? A faith like that may be penetrable.

I'm not saying the object of our faith lets us down, but our connection to him can be knocked a bit off balance if just-getting-by faith is all we strive for. Sometimes folks who had enough faith to just get by walk away from the faith when the first battle came to test them.

Stay connected! The fact that you are reading this right now is a great start. Continue to stay plugged in. What are other ways to connect? Prayer, personal Bible study or with friends, a Time of Grace video or devotion.

When the waves of life hit, and they will, you have the strongest defense. It's not your works, looks, or bank account, which all fail or falter. You have Christ! He's the real superhero, and by faith so are you!

**May 21**

# Your audience of one
### Pastor Daron Lindemann

The audience gathers eagerly. The eighth-grade band students are dressed in their best backstage, nervously waiting for each of their names to be called for a solo performance.

Like professional performers, they will be on stage under the lights all by themselves, and judges will issue a score.

Amber has prepared for this but still feels her nerves fluttering. She paces back and forth until she hears her name. The curtains open, and for a split second she considers turning around and running. She can't do this! She's going to make a mistake!

But she nervously takes center stage and raises her violin.

As she begins, she sees in the audience the smiling, approving face of her mother—no judgment, no fear, just a bunch of mom pride and eager excitement for the best performance in the world.

And that's what Amber does, performs her best in the world. Her mom is her audience of one. When Amber saw her mom, it changed everything.

**"Whatever you do, work at it with all your heart, as working for the Lord, not for human masters. . . . It is the Lord Christ you are serving"** (Colossians 3:23,24).

Serve Jesus as your audience of One in whatever you do.

In mercy he forgives you of everything and smiles approvingly at everything you do for him—no judgment, no fear, just a bunch of heavenly pride and eager excitement for your best performance in the world.

**May 22**

# Free stuff
## Linda Buxa

Every August in Madison, Wisconsin, moving days are a bargain shoppers' dream. As apartment leases end, college students fill the sidewalks and curbs with possessions they no longer want. As the residents are moving out, other people flock in looking for a free dining table or couch or bookshelves or lamp. It's the whole "one man's trash is another man's treasure" concept. People flock to free.

God does this too—except instead of setting out his trash, he gave us his treasure: **"He who did not spare his own Son, but gave him up for us all—how will he not also, along with him, graciously give us all things?"** (Romans 8:32).

God sent Jesus, his own Son, to earth and allowed him to be treated like trash—rejected, scorned, beaten, and crucified in our place. Jesus suffered the punishment we deserved so that God could give us peace, joy, life, and eternity as free gifts.

Because the Father's treasure is now our treasure, it changes how we live: **"Let us run with perseverance the race marked out for us, fixing our eyes on Jesus, the pioneer and perfecter of faith. . . . Consider him who endured such opposition from sinners, so that you will not grow weary and lose heart"** (Hebrews 12:1-3).

**May 23**

# Sitting shotgun with Jesus
## Pastor Mike Novotny

Once upon a time, Jesus pulled a 15-passenger van into a man's driveway. He honked the horn, rolled down the window as the door opened, and smiled, "Hey, it's me, Jesus. I got room if you want."

The man looked around in disbelief, "Me? You're inviting me? Um, yeah! Give me a second to pack all my stuff."

"Oh, wait," Jesus said. "We don't have room for that, but we have room for you. You in?" But the man looked back and saw the home he loved, his leather chair, his new 65" TV, and the evidence of his comfortable life. He glanced back at Jesus, who was still waiting, still smiling, but the man's face fell. Without a word, he quietly closed the door.

Did you know that something like that happened once? You can read the whole story in Mark 10, but here's the saddest part: **"At this the man's face fell. He went away sad, because he had great wealth"** (verse 22).

I won't lie to you. Jesus wants all of you. He wants you to follow him, no matter what dreams, goals, or comforts you might have had before he showed up. This is why so many people break eye contact with Christ and quietly close the door.

But don't! Because Jesus wants you to follow him. He wants your life to be lived at the side of the Son of God and Savior of the world.

What an offer! What a blessing, no matter the cost, to be with Christ!

**May 24**

# Take the world, but give me Jesus
## Pastor David Scharf

It is amazing how many giants of music and the arts today weren't recognized as giants when they were alive. Schubert couldn't find steady employment. Rembrandt died in bankruptcy. Mozart worked himself into a state of sickness that finally killed him. Van Gogh's paintings were spat on by respectable people in his homeland of the Netherlands, and he struggled with poverty.

Jesus is the ultimate example of not being appreciated in his day for who he was: *the* Way, *the* Truth, *the* Life. By and large, Jesus was rejected by his contemporaries, and yet the works of our Savior still change lives and eternities today. Jesus once said of himself, **"The stone the builders rejected has become the cornerstone"** (Luke 20:17). What do you see when you look at Jesus? Do you see the cornerstone that gives direction to the many things in your life, or do you see Jesus as just one of many things that take up your attention in this world?

The reformer Martin Luther had a test to find out if Jesus is really your cornerstone in life. Here it is. When the chips are down in your life, what do you look to for vindication? financial success? family? career? If so, that *underappreciates* what you have in Jesus. Instead, look to the cross. There you find not only your forgiveness but the foundation for every aspect of your life. Take the world, but give me Jesus!

**May 25**

# Seed, sword, Spirit, life
Pastor Mike Novotny

For those who are new to the Old and New Testaments, the Bible might seem like an encyclopedia, a dry and dusty text that people own but rarely read. But the Bible is more. So much more.

The Bible is like a seed, so small you could miss it or entirely dismiss it, yet so packed with potential it could produce, according to Jesus, **"a hundred, sixty or thirty times what was sown"** (Matthew 13:23).

The Bible is like a sword, the weapon that keeps you alive in this spiritual war **"so that you can take your stand against the devil's schemes"** (Ephesians 6:11).

The Bible is full of the Spirit, working invisibly, powerfully, and supernaturally, leading Paul to state that **"faith comes from hearing the message, and the message is heard through the word about Christ"** (Romans 10:17).

The Bible is life itself, prompting Peter to resist the done-with-Jesus crowds and confess, **"Lord, to whom shall we go? You have the words of eternal life"** (John 6:68).

There is no other book that is worthy of so much of your limited time in this life. You are no fool if you begin or end each day (or both!) in the God-breathed, Spirit-filled, life-changing Scriptures.

Because these Scriptures are seed, sword, Spirit, and life.

**May 26**

# The Word is a seed
## Pastor Mike Novotny

I told Ricardo, one of my soccer teammates, about a Bible app that people at my church loved. A year later he said, "Mike, I'm almost done reading the Bible on that app you told me about."

He was in the homestretch of his first-ever time reading the Scriptures! Even better was what he told me about his soul: how the Word had been changing him, especially in his attitude at home and the way he handled stress at work. I was given a fresh reminder that the littlest moments can turn into the biggest blessings in the kingdom of God.

Because God's Word is like a seed. When we read the Bible, hear the Bible, pray the Bible, share the Bible, or discuss the Bible, God is scattering seeds in our hearts. These seeds are potential-packed truths that grow into some of our biggest blessings.

Jesus taught, **"But the seed falling on good soil refers to someone who hears the word and understands it. This is the one who produces a crop, yielding a hundred, sixty or thirty times what was sown"** (Matthew 13:23).

Downloading an app or opening a Bible might seem like a small habit to some, but to those who have tasted and seen that the Lord is good, the Bible is electric in its potential. Today you might read a devotion or get back to Bible-reading, but these are enormously important in the way God works.

Your devotional life might seem small. Seeds are too. But they don't stay that way.

**May 27**

# The Word is a sword
## Pastor Mike Novotny

My friend Ben realized he had forgotten his Bible when we were a state and a half away from home on the way to a Christian conference. To Ben, a Bible-less start to the week was a big problem.

I can see Ben's point. You and I are in a spiritual war against the devil, the world, and our own sinful nature. No wonder Ben wanted a sword in this fight.

**"Take up the shield of faith, with which you can extinguish all the flaming arrows of the evil one. Take the helmet of salvation and the sword of the Spirit, which is the word of God"** (Ephesians 6:16,17).

Imagine hand-to-hand combat without a sword. A helmet and shield would help, but it's hard to win a fight without a sword. Thank God that the Spirit inspired one.

The Bible is the way we battle for God's blessings. When the devil swings his sword of shame at our throats, we raise the Bible and quote, **"There is now no condemnation for those who are in Christ Jesus"** (Romans 8:1). When the father of lies declares we are too far gone for God, we decapitate the deceiver with a Braveheart-esque cry, **"It is by grace [we] have been saved!"** (Ephesians 2:8).

Ben was no fool to fidget without his Bible. Neither are you. Take up the sword of the Spirit, which is the Word of God, and stand your ground today.

**May 28**

# The Word is Spirit
Pastor Mike Novotny

Sometimes I like to think about the connection between eternal treasure, the words of the Bible, and the work of the Spirit. In the epic closing of John 6, our Savior said, **"The words I have spoken to you—they are full of the Spirit"** (verse 63).

If the Bible had a list of ingredients on its back cover, the Holy Spirit would be the first on the list. He fills the pages of Scripture, taking words off a page (or a screen) and planting them like seeds in your heart and your mind. Because he is divinely working, the Bible grabs you in one verse, slaps you to your senses in the next, and allows you to be still and know that he is God before your devotion is over.

Have you experienced this?

Throughout the centuries, humans have sought to find the treasure of God's truth through rituals, pilgrimages, and mountaintop experiences. But our Father, in his mercy, didn't hide the truth about his love and your salvation on the top of Mt. Everest.

Instead, he "hid" it in every Spirit-filled, Christ-centered page of the Holy Bible. We understand what a treasure Jesus is and how much he treasures us when we read his words and listen to our God talk to us over and over again. You may never become a millionaire. But whenever you hold the Scriptures in your hands, you are rich indeed.

**"The law from your mouth is more precious to me than thousands of pieces of silver and gold"** (Psalm 119:72).

**May 29**

# The Word is life
## Pastor Mike Novotny

Somewhere in Somalia, Christians risk their lives to read the Bible. After sunset, a brave disciple retrieves a hidden Bible from a cave, sneaks back into the village, and leads his small group in studying it. Before sunrise, this disciple reverses the process before his neighbors discover the secret and demand his death.

Why take such a risk? Jesus knows: **"The words I have spoken to you—they are full of the Spirit and life"** (John 6:63).

"Life" is one of the ways the Bible talks about being with God. Death is, essentially, distance between you and God, while life is the full enjoyment of his presence.

Without the good news revealed in the Word, no sinner could claim a spot in God's presence. But the words that Jesus spoke are full of life because they are full of access to God. Despite your transgressions, the Bible promises you, a believer in Jesus, the unimaginable—God himself.

Shortly after declaring that the Word of God is **"alive and active,"** the author to the Hebrews writes, **"Let us then approach God's throne of grace with confidence, so that we may receive mercy and find grace to help us in our time of need"** (4:12,16).

Approach the King of kings with confidence. Find mercy for every one of your sins. Find grace. God is not annoyed by your request or bothered by your presence. In fact, he wrote an entire book to tell you just the opposite.

Don't believe me? Read the Word. It is full of the Spirit and life!

**May 30** | Memorial Day

## Taps
Christine Wentzel

"Taps is a military bugle call played slow and solemn to invoke a feeling of remembrance and respect for the soldiers who have died in battle. On a trumpet, there are no valve movements, only tone changes made with the pursing of the lips" (*Naval Bugler*, 1974).

This haunting tune and loud rifle volleys echoed within our heavy hearts as we drove away from our family's funeral service in Arlington National Cemetery. We viewed orderly rows of identical white headstones. The only marked difference was an engraved religious affiliation symbol.

There are faith stories behind those fallen saints with crosses on their stones.

It is said there are no atheists in foxholes. Whether in hell on the front lines or in the PTSD mind, "Oh God!" was a common cry among sinner and saint alike. From the saint to the sinner came the gift to share the divine comfort about their personal rescue from eternal death. Out of love, God sent his Son. The gift of faith and a rebirth in the Holy Spirit awaited their confession from a repentant heart. In that moment of grace, the sinner became the saint and eventually arrived safely in heaven.

We will never forget your sacrificial service to God and country.

>Onward, then, ye faithful; join the happy throng,
>Blend with ours your voices in the triumph song:
>Glory, laud, and honor unto Christ the King;
>This through countless ages saints and angels sing.
>
>                    ("Onward Christian Soldiers")

**May 31**

# Overflowing
## Pastor Daron Lindemann

"Excuse me, sir?!" I was trying to exit a coffee shop as a kind lady behind the coffee bar continued, "I was listening to your Bible study about the Holy Spirit."

Apparently, the awkwardness of eavesdropping didn't concern her. She launched into her faith story while mixing up a latte. She quickly reviewed her upbringing as sad, abusive, and relying on addiction to numb the pain. These behaviors continued into her adult years, but four years ago she got in some trouble and God rescued her.

Throughout this story, she never stopped smiling and never stopped steaming the milk. She wasn't ashamed. She wasn't a victim looking for sympathy. She cared more about God and his words coming to life in her than she cared about anything else in that moment. She was consumed by it. Captivated by the One who changed her life, forgave her, loved her, freed her.

And she had to tell me about it. Just because. Like coffee aroma always overflows through the shop.

People whose lives have been transformed by God's Word and work just have to talk about it. Today, live up to these words, telling God that this is what you want to do:

**"My soul is consumed with longing for your laws at all times. Your statutes are my delight. . . . Never take your word of truth from my mouth. . . . See how I love your precepts; preserve my life, Lord, in accordance with your love."** (Psalm 119:20,24,43,159)

# JUNE

Whether you eat or drink or whatever you do, do it all for the glory of God.

1 CORINTHIANS 10:31

**June 1**

# If things are going well
## Pastor Mike Novotny

If things are going well in this season of your spiritual life, I want to praise God with you. And I want to quote God to warn you.

God once said, **"So, if you think you are standing firm, be careful that you don't fall!"** (1 Corinthians 10:12). Sometimes success makes us feel like we're standing so firm that we don't need to be careful anymore. We can forget that God blessed us with success *because* we were working his steps to victory.

Have you ever met someone who decided to stop taking their medication because they were feeling mentally healthy? They forgot that they are healthy *because of* the medication.

Have you ever met a teenager who was raised in the church and decided that they didn't need to attend while in college because their faith was so strong? They forgot that they were strong *because of* church.

Don't take that bait when it comes to your spiritual habits. If you have a few weeks of obedience under your belt, praise God and keep working the steps. If praying, confessing, and filling your heart with the Word has been working, then keep doing what's been working.

Stand firm in the process that God is using to produce the fruit of self-control in you. That is how you stay standing and avoid an unexpected fall.

**June 2**

# If things aren't going well
Pastor Mike Novotny

If things aren't going well in this season of your spiritual life, I want to grieve with you. And I want to quote God to encourage you:

**"As the rain and the snow come down from heaven, and do not return to it without watering the earth and making it bud and flourish, so that it yields seed for the sower and bread for the eater, so is my word that goes out from my mouth: It will not return to me empty, but will accomplish what I desire and achieve the purpose for which I sent it"** (Isaiah 55:10,11).

Sometimes failure makes us feel like the Word is not working. But God often is working in ways our eyes cannot see.

If someone told you that snow produces grain, you might laugh. The snow falls and sits and melts and . . . nothing. But beneath the surface, the melted snow is soaking into the soil and preparing the ground for the seeds that are soon to come.

Your journey with Christian living is like that. You might not see immediate results. All these devotions about God's love and the power of prayer might not produce instant change. But God swears that his Word "will not return to me empty."

Yesterday's message might be exactly what you need two months from now. Last week's devotion might pop into your head in a fierce moment of temptation or a lonely evening of self-loathing. The Word is working. It has to. God said it.

And God never lies to his children.

**June 3**

# Keep the party going
## Pastor Clark Schultz

Is there a party in your future? A graduation, wedding, anniversary, or retirement? Do you know what makes a party successful? Planning, people, some presents, and quality entertainment.

God planned the birthday of his New Testament Christian church with all the same elements in place. Ten days after Jesus went up to heaven, folks from all over the Mediterranean gathered in Jerusalem for the Old Testament harvest festival. Here God had the Holy Spirit come on his disciples, and they were able to speak in other languages. We call this Pentecost in the Christian church. A crowd heard the disciples and were amazed: **"Then how is it that each of us hears them in our native language?** (Acts 2:8).

What do you think happened next? Those folks heard the gospel for the first time in their own language and took it back to their homelands. The gospel spread like fire. How far? All the way to you, dear reader. The challenge for you and me is this: can we keep the fire burning and the party going? Some that Pentecost morning felt this was a gimmick or the disciples were drunk. We too can slip into excuse after excuse of why it is someone else's job to spread the Word.

Party checklist requirements: 1) you have an awesome God who loves you and equips you with unique gifts, and 2) more important, you have the same Holy Spirit who gives you power through the Word. So keep the Pentecost party going!

**June 4**

# You are the plan
## Pastor David Scharf

There is an old legend—and I stress it is merely a legend—that illustrates a good point. The legend is that after Jesus ascended into heaven, the angel Gabriel asked him, "Who is going to carry on your work now?" And Jesus answered, "I have left it to John and Peter and Andrew and the others." Gabriel then asked, "What if they don't do it?" Jesus answered, "I have made no other plans."

In other words, you and I are the plan. Jesus said, "*You* will be my witnesses." He does not use angels; he uses us. Why? Because the angels have never known what it is like to be forgiven, to go from hell to heaven in a moment. We do. So did Isaiah the prophet. Isaiah thought he was going to die, but God forgave his sin. Isaiah records: **"Then I heard the voice of the Lord saying, 'Whom shall I send? And who will go for us?' And I said, 'Here am I. Send me!'"** (Isaiah 6:8). Isaiah went from "Woe is me" to "Here am I. Send me!"

Jesus came to pay for your sin with his life and death. Jesus suffered hell so that heaven is now yours. Jesus lives to bless you today beyond all that you ask or imagine. Jesus is with *you*. Now he asks, "Who will go for me?" What else can you do but respond, "Send me!" After all, you are the plan!

**June 5**

# Don't forget to breathe
Pastor Clark Schultz

Somewhere between a pike press, a plank, and high knees, the instructor shouted, "Don't forget to breathe!"

"Who's the idiot who forgets to breathe?" I wondered.

Mere moments later, I was the one feeling light-headed and dizzy. Yup, you guessed it; I didn't breathe.

When you exercise and your muscles work harder, your body uses more oxygen and produces more carbon dioxide. To cope with this extra demand, your breathing has to increase from about 15 times a minute when you are resting to up to 40 to 60 times a minute during exercise.

Life is a series of breaths. From the moment God created man—**"the Lord God . . . breathed into his nostrils the breath of life, and the man became a living being"** (Genesis 2:7)—to when we take our last breath, a **"person's days are determined"** (Job 14:5).

But what about all the days in between? Stress, work, family, depression—many times we want to hold our breath. Spiritually, physically, and mentally we become light-headed. When those moments come, don't hold it in. Take a breath and let it all out on God because he reminds us to **"call on [him] in the day of trouble"** (Psalm 50:15).

Deep breath in and now out . . . God's got this.

**June 6**

# Good enough for God?
Pastor Mike Novotny

About ten years ago, I met a young woman who was a good person. I mean, a really good person. One of those people who got along with everyone at her high school—the athletes, the musicians, the math kids, everyone. Soon after we met, I asked her if she thought she was good enough to get into heaven. "I'm not sure," she confessed. But she came to church and then to Bible class, listening to Jesus' words, his standards, and his promises. Not long after, I asked her the same question I had posed months earlier: "Are you good enough to go to heaven?"

"Oh, I'm sure," she smiled, a smile that reflected a change that had happened in her heart. She met Jesus, the real Jesus, the only Jesus who could make her not just good but Good, Good enough for God.

The earliest Christians put it this way: **"Salvation is found in no one else, for there is no other name under heaven given to mankind by which we must be saved"** (Acts 4:12). They believed that there was one name that could save them, the name of Jesus Christ their King.

So are you good enough for heaven? Good enough to have God think about you and smile? Good enough to live in his presence both now and forever? Through Jesus, the answer is an undeniable Yes! His name was given so that we could be saved from every spiritual danger and enjoy every spiritual blessing. What a name!

## Pop-up storms
Andrea Delwiche

Have you experienced a pop-up storm on a sunny summer day? Within a few moments, your activities must change as you respond to new conditions.

Each day of our lives contains pop-up storms of different magnitudes. And our outlook may suddenly shift too, making each situation loom large. As believers, we are not immune from suffering or anxiety. We may bob in a sea of despair, each wave threatening to fill our lungs with water as we pray for breath to survive.

But we don't need to face life barely treading water. **"Blessed be the Lord, who daily bears us up; God is our salvation"** (Psalm 68:19 ESV). The Lord comes beneath us and "bears us up" so that we don't drown. And while Jesus very clearly tells his followers, **"In this world you will have troubles"** (John 16:33), he also reassures us, **"Peace I leave with you; my peace I give you. . . . Do not let your hearts be troubled and do not be afraid"** (John 14:27).

God is our salvation. We share in Christ's resurrection and will live with him forever. God is also our salvation in the nitty-gritty of daily life. He wants to lead us into the way of love and trust as we come to understand his steadfast character, praise him, and work with him to bless others.

What evidence of God's support can you see when you examine the last 24 hours? God is daily investing in and supporting the well-being of your body and soul.

**June 8**

# Blink first
## Christine Wentzel

If you've lived long enough and squabbled often enough, you know by now that pride starts every conflict but never ends it. By nature, we thrive on pride. Nothing stirs that dark nature more than seeing someone we don't like getting something we believe is undeserved. In friendships, we keep mental scorecards on our giving and their taking. It takes a confrontation on pride for humility to win, and that conflict ended in victory two thousand-plus years ago.

It took an incredible act of love on God's part to win that war. Jesus chose to blink first by laying aside his all-encompassing sovereignty and become small enough to fit into the confines of bones and flesh. He overcame every temptation the devil could throw at him. He intentionally allowed himself to be crucified by the very people he came to save. He defeated death by rising from the grave. His victory makes us free and eager to blink first in any stare down to joyfully show the character of true love.

Not budging an inch with your spouse? Blink first.

Not seeing eye to eye on a church issue? Blink first.

Haven't talked to a friend in a long time? Blink first.

Won't take the garbage out because it's not your turn? Blink first.

**"Therefore if you have any encouragement from being united with Christ, if any comfort from his love, if any common sharing in the Spirit, if any tenderness and compassion, then make my joy complete by being like-minded, having the same love, being one in spirit and of one mind"** (Philippians 2:1,2).

June 9

## They sharpen you
Pastor Mike Novotny

By nature, we become dull. Just ask the knives in your kitchen drawer. As time passes and meals are made, they don't naturally become sharper but instead lose their edge. To stay sharp, they need to be acted upon aggressively by an outside force.

The same is true for you. By nature, we become dull to the realities of God, forgetting how glorious he is, how serious sin is, and how loved we are. Like a farmer working in a cow barn who has gotten used to the smell or a woman who lives by the ocean and is no longer moved by its beauty, we too can grow complacent. We forget.

This is why we need Christian friends. The classic proverb reminds us, **"As iron sharpens iron, so one person sharpens another"** (Proverbs 27:17). I love that picture. To stay sharp and effective, an iron tool needs the help of another iron tool. For Christians to stay sharp in their thinking and effective in their living, we need the help of other Christians.

Today is a great day to ask someone to keep you sharp. Have the courage to ask them, "What do other people think of me? What don't I see?" Warning—The answers might cause some friction. But please remember that it takes some friction for dull things to become sharp again.

Friend, your life matters. The way you live matters. May God give you the humility to ask honest questions, to consider candid answers, and to stay sharp in your faith.

**June 10**

# Lost in translation
## Pastor Clark Schultz

A few years back, I took a trip to Germany. In addition to the historic sites, the food was amazing. I'm not sure if you know this, but in Germany most folks speak German. Kidding aside . . . there were moments, when asking in my broken German, that simple phrases like "where is the bathroom" or "may I have an ice cream cone" got lost in translation. I knew what I wanted. The person on the other side of my conversation knew what he or she wanted, but we just couldn't communicate it clearly.

Biblically that is true too. God loves us. God wants us to have a relationship with him, but due to sin, it gets lost in translation. We have our own pity parties, make God out to be a bad guy, and think that God just doesn't care about us.

When Jesus prayed to heal a deaf man, this phrase stands out: **"He looked up to heaven and with a *deep sigh* . . ."** (Mark 7:34). This was not a father frustrated with his children sigh. This sigh was similar to the tears Jesus shed at his friend's funeral or the compassion he showed to the widow who lost her only son. It's the same empathy he shows to you. His heart goes out to you. Jesus is not some far-removed God who is too busy to know or care about you. He gave his life for you!

**"Because he himself suffered when he was tempted, he is able to help those who are being tempted"** (Hebrews 2:18).

**June 11**

# The dumpster story
Pastor Mike Novotny

There was once a man who had a secret stash of pornographic magazines. One day when his wife was gone, he indulged his sinful nature but immediately felt the shame of his hypocrisy. So he took the whole stack of magazines down to the dumpster for their apartment complex and threw them away once and for all.

Well, not exactly once and for all. Something within him didn't want to give up those fleeting moments of pleasure, so before his wife returned, the man decided he would get the magazines back. He reached over the edge and—ready for this?—fell headfirst and broke his arm, leaving him stuck at the bottom of the dumpster and unable to escape until his wife came home.

Seriously. That happened.

Any sin, on its worst days, can feel like that. You love it, you hate it, you love it again, and you sometimes end up broken and bottomed out. There are moments when there are no logical explanations for our sin, just the intense shame of our addictive choices.

This is why Romans 5:20 is worth memorizing: **"But where sin increased, grace increased all the more."** When your sin feels so overwhelmingly big, remember what is always bigger—the grace of God. When our Father finds you in the dumpster of immorality, he doesn't walk away in disgust. Instead, he offers a hand, cleans you up, and stays by your side to nurse you back to health.

He cares that much. He is a perfect Father after all.

**June 12**

# Get in the wheelbarrow
## Pastor Jon Enter

Where are you struggling to trust the power and protection of God?

Years ago a tightrope walker did amazing stunts at tremendously scary heights in Paris. An American promoter doubted his ability and challenged him to tightrope walk over Niagara Falls. He did. Then the daredevil walked the tightrope again blindfolded and pushing a wheelbarrow. He asked the promoter, "Now do you believe I can do it?"

"Yes, of course," the promoter said.

"Good!" the stuntman replied. "Then get in the wheelbarrow!"

It's one thing to say, "I trust you." It's entirely different to have your life and well-being directly in the hands of another.

It's one thing to say, "God, I love you." It's entirely different to have your life and your eternity in the hands of Jesus. James challenges you to go beyond words in expressing your faith: **"Faith without deeds is dead. . . . I will show you my faith by my deeds"** (James 2:26,18).

Jesus is the object of your faith, but what is the objective of your faith? Get in God's wheelbarrow (so to speak), and trust God will not let you fall. If he has power to create wind and the gentleness to calm its force, if he has power to destroy the grip of death and the gentleness to dry the tears of those who weep, he has the power to protect you and the gentleness to comfort you. Nothing is too big or too small for his love.

**June 13**

# Trash talk?
## Pastor Daron Lindemann

I was bullied as a kid. He would stalk me after school and trash-talk: "I'm gonna punch you in the face!" I was too scared to trash-talk back.

Learn to be a better trash-talker. Why? Because your fiercest enemies are trash-talking all the time. If you listen to them, you will lose.

The Bible teaches you to respond with trash talk of your own and put these enemies in their place. Well, it's really not trash talk but truth talk because it comes from God.

Here it is: **"'Where, O death, is your victory? Where, O death, is your sting?' The sting of death is sin, and the power of sin is the law. But thanks be to God! He gives us the victory through our Lord Jesus Christ"** (1 Corinthians 15:55-57).

Take a cue from the Bible here for some truth talk!

"Hey, sin, Jesus died and rose so you can't curse me, you don't make me dirty, and Jesus' empty tomb empowers me to say no to you, sin!"

"Hey, death, do you really think you win? Jesus rose, and you are dead. New life from Jesus with my name on it is in charge, and I'm going to live that life now and in heaven!"

"Hey, devil, sure you're real, but I'm not afraid of you trying to intimidate me and manipulate me. You are full of lies, but Jesus is my truth and life. He is Lord, not you!"

**June 14**

# You must not love God enough
Linda Buxa

A friend was going through a really hard time and told me some of the "encouragement" she received from other Christians. "You didn't have enough faith." "If you had been in a closer relationship with God, this wouldn't have happened." "You must not be praying hard enough."

Those comments reminded me of a Bible story involving a man who was born blind. "[Jesus'] **disciples asked him, 'Rabbi, who sinned, this man or his parents, that he was born blind?' 'Neither this man nor his parents sinned,' said Jesus, 'but this happened so that the works of God might be displayed in him'"** (John 9:1-3).

When we look for reasons why bad things happen to other people, it's like we are asking the same question as those in Jesus' inner circle: Who sinned?

I think we say those things because if we can find a reason why bad things happen, then we can take action to ensure they won't happen to us. The truth is simply that in a world that is no longer perfect (the way God created it to be), bad things will happen to "good" people.

This means that bad things will happen to you and me too.

Instead of asking who sinned and accusing the people around you of not praying or believing enough, we simply sit by them, hug them, and remind them that even if we don't know what God is doing, we trust that God's work will be displayed in their lives.

**June 15**

# Best chapter ever?
Pastor Mike Novotny

In the early 1600s, Thomas Goodwin, an English preacher, wrote a lot of words about God. A lot of words. When put together, Goodwin's work filled 12 volumes, over 500 pages each, in small font with the lines squished together. But volume 2 was the most interesting. In volume 2, Goodwin didn't cover 1/12th of the Bible, as you might logically assume. Nor did he narrow his focus to one book of the Bible. Instead, Goodwin spent an entire volume, 500 tiny printed pages, trying to explain just one chapter of the Bible! Which chapter was that? Ephesians chapter 2.

Have you read it? You should. If you wonder why the world is so messed up, why people are so messed up, or why you sometimes are so messed up, it's in Ephesians chapter 2. And if you want to know how to fix it, you won't need to turn the page. If your life could use a little more grace, mercy, and kindness, leave your bookmark in the same place because Paul is proud to cover that too.

I don't have room to reprint the whole chapter here, but let me inspire you to open your own Bible to that epic page by quoting these epic words: **"Like the rest, we were by nature deserving of wrath. But because of his great love for us, God, who is rich in mercy, made us alive with Christ even when we were dead in transgressions—it is by grace you have been saved"** (Ephesians 2:3-5).

**June 16**

## Pray the psalms
Andrea Delwiche

"Make haste, O God, to deliver me! O Lord, make haste to help me! Let them be put to shame and confusion who seek my life! Let them be turned back and brought to dishonor who delight in my hurt! Let them turn back because of their shame who say, 'Aha, Aha!' May all who seek you rejoice and be glad in you! May those who love your salvation say evermore, 'God is great!' But I am poor and needy; hasten to me, O God! You are my help and my deliverer; O Lord, do not delay!" (Psalm 70 ESV).

The words of this ancient psalm are compact and suitable to the daily challenges we face. Each day we need God's deliverance and protection. Each day we have reason to rejoice in God's greatness.

Early Christians and some Christians still today memorize psalms to use as prayers. Christ himself certainly knew the psalms by heart and used them as he battled temptation. He used the psalms to express his heart to his Father as he hung on a cross.

For us also the psalms can be prayers ready for us not only in moments of crisis but as blessings to pray over our ordinary moments. Situations change, but God's faithfulness and eagerness to spend time with us and to rescue us is new each day.

## We're no angels
Christine Wentzel

"Do not fail to show love to strangers, for by doing this some have welcomed angels without realizing it" (Hebrews 13:2 EHV).

"BC" was a societal outcast; an older man with untreated mental illness, stronghold addictions, and physical disabilities. He was homely, disheveled, and unwashed. He was prone to angry outbursts and untethered joy. He possessed an infectious smile overlaying dirty teeth. He was outwardly unique in our Christian congregation. Was he our visiting angel?

Soon after my prodigal return, God worked on my residual worldliness. BC was one of many faith-building lessons. When I first spotted BC, I had a knee-jerk, sin-filled reaction of distaste. One Sunday service, I walked passed him to reach the very last pew. It was empty enough to accommodate my personal space from the rest of the flock. Just as I settled in, BC climbed over me, sat at my hip, and grabbed the hymnal out of my hands. My eyes watered from the alcoholic fumes; I was ready to bolt. Suddenly, Hebrews 13:2 spoke as a whispered memory and instantly convicted my pride-filled heart.

"God, forgive me for this sin of self-righteousness. Help me see BC as you see him, as you see me. Help me love BC as you love him, as you love me. Amen."

I turned to face BC and asked, "Will you share that hymnal with me?" Together we worshiped our triune God. We were no angels. We were a family in Christ. We learned and grew under God's care. One day we will be united in heaven and live in loving harmony forever.

**June 18**

## God is with us
Andrea Delwiche

Life continues day in and day out, morning and evening. Seasons emerge and fade. Leaves color and fall and then months later slowly emerge. Children are born and grow. Our family members grow old and leave us. Power is accumulated and disintegrates. Governments rise and fall. Illness has us in its grip and then loosens its hold. We savor tears of joy and are caught in the grasp of grief. The words of Ecclesiastes 3:1 resonate with nearly everyone: **"To every thing there is a season, and a time to every purpose under the heaven"** (KJV).

We can feel powerless in our own lives, unable to stop time, unable to effect change, unable to pursue the good that needs to be done for Christ, for our neighbors, for our families. "Who is in control?" we ask. "Who is working for us?"

The confession of this psalmist, writing during the destruction of every other certainty, can be our hope as well: **"For God is my King of old, working salvation in the midst of the earth"** (Psalm 74:12 KJV). Can you stop for a minute and focus on this certainty? Can you picture it in your head? Our God—Father, Son, and Spirit, who spoke our world into being—still stands in our midst, protecting, guiding, working. As his beloved child, he holds you close to him.

God is never absent from his earth. He who formed it continues working in it, alongside and on behalf of his beloved people. His arm is strong. His wisdom is unsurpassable. His goodness never ends.

Father's Day | **June 19**

## Dads on duty
Linda Buxa

At Southwood High School in Shreveport, Louisiana, 23 students were arrested over the course of three days due to violent fights at school. About 40 dads decided to step up to be part of the solution. "We're dads. We decided the best people who can take care of our kids are who? Are us," said father Michael LaFitte. Calling themselves Dads on Duty, these men take turns spending time at school, encouraging the students and helping maintain a positive environment. They've turned the school from a fight club into a refuge. "I immediately felt a form of safety," one of the students said. "The school has just been happy—and you can feel it," said another.*

Today is the day in the United States that we set aside to honor fathers and recognize the vital role they play in the lives of children. Science shows that children who have a father present have higher rates of performance at school, tend to excel in their careers, have elevated levels of physical and mental health, become better problem-solvers, are more confident and empathetic, and are more economically stable. In addition, their communities are safer, as the Dads on Duty showed.

Children who have a father who believes in Jesus also receive the best positive impact of all: **"Whoever fears the Lord has a secure fortress, and for their children it will be a refuge"** (Proverbs 14:26).

Thanks, dads, for being on duty, for creating a place of both physical and spiritual refuge for children!

*https://www.cbsnews.com/news/dads-louisiana-high-school-student-violence/

**June 20**

# Being a Christian is hard!
## Pastor David Scharf

"Why is my life as a Christian so hard? It wasn't this hard before." That has been spoken or thought by many new Christians. Maybe you've thought it too. Before there was no pang of conscience when you did whatever made you happy. There were no strange looks, but now you see them on your friends' faces when you go to church. There were no conflicts in your conversations, but now you feel the "archaic" and "close-minded" labels being pinned to your back because of Scripture. You realize that striving to please self (before) was a whole lot easier than striving to please Jesus (now). Being a Christian is hard.

Jesus said as much. **"For whoever wants to save their life will lose it, but whoever loses their life for me will find it"** (Matthew 16:25). A wise theologian once commented, "When Christ calls a man, he bids him to come and die." In other words, the more I live in Christ's words, the more I die and the more he lives in me. That's the goal of the Christian life. I want my weakness, my sin, my insecurity, my _____ to die. In its place Jesus fills me with his strength, his forgiveness, the confidence that comes from him, and . . . ultimately, he exchanges the cross I carry in this life as a Christian for the crown of heaven.

So, yes, being a Christian is hard but worth it! God's blessings as you lose *your* life today and find it *in Christ*.

**June 21**

# Stop playing it safe
Pastor Daron Lindemann

I am a safety-holic and don't take enough risks. I asked some guys at church if they wear safety glasses for yard chores like I do. They kinda looked at me funny.

Okay, so I need to skip my vitamins once in a while. I need to talk to people about Jesus with more passion and less concern that they'll look at me funny. I need to trust Jesus more and my own control and comfort less. You need to trust Jesus more too. He called his disciples not to a sterilized, quarantined safety zone but to a stormy, life-changing mission.

Jesus appeared to his disciples, seeking safety in a locked room after he had died. **"'As the Father has sent me, I am sending you.' And with that he breathed on them and said, 'Receive the Holy Spirit. If you forgive anyone's sins, their sins are forgiven; if you do not forgive them, they are not forgiven'"** (John 20:21-23).

Will Jesus' mission for you be safe? Actually, it will be a whole lot safer than you locking down the status quo and staying tied down to what makes you comfortable (so that you don't need Jesus).

Jesus gives you three reasons to take more God-honoring risks for him. He is sending you so the mission is holy. He gives you the Holy Spirit so that God himself is in you. People need forgiveness, and you can assure them of it.

Stop playing it safe!

**June 22**

# Billy Graham, a glimpse of God
Pastor Mike Novotny

Billy Graham's daughter Ruth, in her book on forgiveness, recounts the day when her father gave her a stunning glimpse of our Father.

After a messy divorce, Ruth fell in love again. Her children didn't like her new boyfriend, and her parents had deep concerns. But after only six months of knowing this new man, Ruth followed her heart and married him. A day after their vows, however, she realized she had made a mistake, finally seeing the red flags that others had pointed out. She moved out within weeks, knowing the marriage was over.

She knew she had to drive home and face her parents. Ruth tells the story: "As I rounded the last bend in my parents' driveway, I saw my father standing there, waiting for me. . . . As I turned off the ignition, Daddy approached. I opened the car door and . . . he spread his long arms wide, wrapped me in his tight embrace, and said, 'Welcome home.' . . . I was wrapped in grace. Unmerited. Undeserved. Merciful. Generous. Billy Graham was not God, but he modeled God's grace for me. Never again would the theological definition of *grace* be just an academic concept for me. It was now a personal experience" (From *Forgiving My Father, Forgiving Myself*, p.74).

How incredible to feel a glimpse of God's amazing heart. **"Praise be to the God and Father of our Lord Jesus Christ, the Father of compassion and the God of all comfort"** (2 Corinthians 1:3).

**June 23**

## An acceptable time
Andrea Delwiche

God has a particular plan in mind for each of us. He always works the circumstances in our lives for good. Sometimes it can be hard to see the good immediately. But waiting on God and his timing is much easier when we trust him—when we know that although we are dangling out over the ledge of life, God has us by the hand and won't let us go.

In Psalm 69:13, David wrote, **"But as for me, my prayer is to you, O Lord. At an acceptable time, O God, in the abundance of your steadfast love answer me in your saving faithfulness"** (ESV). His trust in God was strong, even during severe trials, because the foundational work of building a relationship with God had been done. David had practiced meditating on the works and promises of God. He knew that the deliverance and the answers he sought would come from God "at an acceptable time."

Try spending a few minutes with this section of Scripture. Let your mind and heart stay with it. Read it again and start to picture what these words meant to David, what his frame of mind might have been as he was writing them. Read it a third time and consider how these words can bring comfort and understanding to your own life. This is your own foundation work.

Ask God to let his words soak into your soul. Talk with God about the ways you are trying to understand his "acceptable time" in your life. May your time together be blessed!

**June 24**

# Get dressed!
## Pastor Clark Schultz

Get dressed! This phrase starts and ends our days. Children fighting to take off their pajamas in the A.M. are arguing 12 hours later to put those same pj's back on at the end of the day. "Why is it always a fight?" my wife and I ask.

The world is evil, and for the Christian there is always a fight. The apostle Paul tells us in Ephesians 6:11-17 to get dressed. But what do we wear? Paul has excellent fashion advice. **"The helmet of salvation"**: where your head goes, you go. Is your head on straight? Perhaps life makes you shake your head, but you are saved! No matter what happens, God has saved you! Let that soak into your head.

**"The breastplate of righteousness"**: a breastplate protects the vital organs. Many in this world will take their stab at you, ridicule you, or try to tear you down. You are right with God! Christ made you righteous no matter what others hurl at you.

**"The belt of truth"**: a belt holds up and holds close. You want the truth? God in his Word holds you up! God through his Son's sacrifice holds you close.

Finally, **"your feet fitted with . . . readiness"**: where you go, there you are. Your mission in life is not to get rich or die trying. Whatever occupation, whatever road you are on, you take the gospel with you to share with others. This peace you have of sins forgiven can be shared with others who need to get dressed!

**June 25**

# Why Paul loved grace (and we do too)
Pastor Mike Novotny

The apostle Paul was the poster child for grace. If the internet would have been invented two thousand years earlier, he immediately would have reserved the website grace.com. If Paul would have gotten married and been blessed with daughters, I bet he would have named them Grace, Gracie, and Baby Grae-Grae.

Why do I think that? Check out this data—Paul wrote 28% of the total words of the New Testament (he wrote 13 of the 27 books, but they're often rather short). Yet Paul is responsible for 73% of the occurrences of the word *grace* in the New Testament! Of the 114 total occurrences of *grace*, 83 of them are from Paul. In fact, every letter that Paul wrote starts with grace and ends with, you got it, more grace. An editor might have encouraged him to spice up his writing with a few synonyms, but Paul insisted in book after book and verse after verse on talking about the grace of our Lord Jesus Christ.

Here's why: **"But by the grace of God I am what I am, and his grace to me was not without effect"** (1 Corinthians 15:10). Grace both made Paul and changed Paul. Grace was his everything.

Meditate on the meaning of grace, and you might feel the same way. Undeserved love. God's smile when you assume he would scowl. Favor and blessing, even if you've fallen and blown it. Picture God's face, shining upon you because of Jesus, and you'll get addicted to grace too.

**June 26**

# Can I trust God's power?
Pastor David Scharf

"I trust God, but some things just seem insurmountable even for God." You have probably never said it out loud, but we have all thought it. The evidence is that we doubt and worry. But does it even make sense to worry? God is the One who made *everything*, and he is in control of *everything*. So what are we really worried about? I suppose we are worried not so much that God doesn't have the power but that he doesn't love me enough to use that power for me. Look at the cross and see God's love for you. The One who invested his own blood in your salvation is not going to withhold his power from you!

Do you remember Gideon? Unsure Gideon needed assurance after assurance. God told a trembling Gideon, **"With the three hundred men . . . I will save you and give the Midianites into your hands"** (Judges 7:7). Someone once said that "with a penny I can do nothing, but with God and a penny there is nothing I cannot do." How do you think Gideon felt in the book of Judges with an army of 300 going up against an army of 450,000? That 300 must have felt like he had a penny, but he trusted God's power. And you can too. Just look at Jesus' love for you on the cross for the proof that there is nothing he is not willing to do for you! You can trust God's power!

**June 27**

# The best version of you
### Pastor Daron Lindemann

You are the best version of yourself when you believe that what God says about you is true.

When you consume others' social media posts and compare yourself to them or you accept the powerful propaganda that only you can decide your identity—this is not your best identity.

Instead, praise God for designing you: **"You created my inmost being; you knit me together in my mother's womb"** (Psalm 139:13).

My college roommate had an afghan blanket knitted by his mom. Woven into it were all his favorite sports, hobbies, nicknames, family names, and some dates. Nobody else fit under that blanket. It was uniquely him.

God knit into you everything that is uniquely you . . . with no mistakes. God brought into being his version of you.

**"My frame was not hidden from you when I was made in the secret place, when I was woven together in the depths of the earth"** (Psalm 139:15). "The depths of the earth" is ancient language saying, "That's so far away nobody knows how to get there except God."

It's an intimate, secret place where it was only God and you. He didn't check Pinterest. He didn't Google nose shapes or personality mixes. Secret. Just you and God. His eyes were only on you.

There and then he created, designed, sculpted, and brought into this world his version of you. Which is the best version of you. And nobody is a better you than you! So. Be. You.

**June 28**

# They comfort you
Pastor Mike Novotny

Have you read the the *Scarlet Letter*? A woman named Hester is pregnant; no one knows the identity of the father except Hester and the pastor. Too ashamed to confess his sin, the pastor smiles and preaches, but the secret of his affair kills him inside. He can't live with the lie but is afraid to speak the truth. In my favorite quote, the pastor says, *"Had I one friend . . . to whom . . . I could daily [go to], and be known as the vilest of all sinners, [I think] my soul might keep itself alive."*

That quote brings me to tears, not because I have had an affair but because I know how good it is to have friends like that. God has surrounded me with a small group of Christians who know me fully yet love me completely. I can tell them I am a sinner, the vilest sinner I know, and yet they don't run away. They listen. They love. They bring me back to Jesus.

Do you have friends like that? James writes, **"Therefore confess your sins to each other and pray for each other so that you may be healed"** (5:16). While God loves to hear our honest confessions, he also loves overhearing our confessions to others, an act that allows fellow believers to imitate our Father and forgive us completely.

It's hard to preach the gospel to yourself, but it is easy for them. Tell them what happened. Then listen when they tell you what happened at the cross.

**June 29**

# But I
Pastor Mike Novotny

There are three words that have changed my life in amazing ways—*GOD is here!* But there are two words that have changed my life in agonizing ways—*But I*.

*But I* is my two-word description of what the Bible calls our "flesh" or "sinful nature." Paul writes, **"All of us also lived among them at one time, gratifying the cravings of our flesh and following its desires and thoughts"** (Ephesians 2:3). The human problem is that our flesh has thoughts, desires, and cravings and we tend to follow and gratify them. God says _____, and we respond with, "But I . . ."

Love your neighbor. "But I don't like him." Honor your father. "But I don't think he's worthy of honor." Forgive 77 times. "But I have the right to be bitter." Flee from sexual immorality. "But I have needs." Don't let unwholesome talk come out of your mouth. "But I need to vent sometimes."

*But I.* Those two words can kill you because they separate you from the God who is life. This is why I want to encourage you today to call out your flesh. When you find yourself thinking in opposition to God, repeating the devil's absurd claim that God is wrong (Genesis 3:4), drag your flesh into the light before it's too late.

The flesh can kill you. But God is in the business of making you alive. **"But because of his great love for us, God, who is rich in mercy, made us alive with Christ"** (Ephesians 2:4,5).

**June 30**

# A double-edged sword
## Pastor Clark Schultz

A parody of the game show *Jeopardy* had guests who were not the brightest misreading the categories, much to the frustration of the host. One category in particular was (S) words, and the guests kept saying, "I'll take Swords for $400, Alex."

The apostle Paul reminds us to take a sword—**"the sword of the Spirit"** (Ephesians 6:17). This is our offensive weapon. We use this to pierce the hearts of others with God's law and God's gospel. A seminary professor told me both law and gospel need to be there, like wings on an airplane. You can only get so far with one wing on an airplane.

Some think speaking the law isn't loving. But nothing could be further from the truth. If I let my kids do whatever they want, while I may win "Coolest Dad of the Year," I will not be showing them love because it may cause them more harm than good. Also, to take the law out of the equation is to forget why we need a Savior. If we don't need Jesus, what's the point of his suffering and dying?

As I write this, our society is hurling (s) words, four-letter words, and you name it. Perhaps it is time that Christians share this sharper double-edged sword (Hebrews 4:12), showing others their sins in a truthful and loving way. More important, showing them their Savior because that is the best parting gift one could have in this game called life.

# About the Writers

**Pastor Mike Novotny** has served God's people in full-time ministry since 2007 in Madison and, most recently, at The CORE in Appleton, Wisconsin. He also serves as the lead speaker for Time of Grace, where he shares the good news about Jesus through television, print, and online platforms. Mike loves seeing people grasp the depth of God's amazing grace and unstoppable mercy. His wife continues to love him (despite plenty of reasons not to), and his two daughters open his eyes to the love of God for every Christian. When not talking about Jesus or dating his wife/girls, Mike loves playing soccer, running, and reading.

**Linda Buxa** is a freelance writer and Bible study leader. She is a regular speaker at women's retreats and conferences across the country, as well as a regular blogger and contributing writer for Time of Grace Ministry. Linda is the author of *Dig In! Family Devotions to Feed Your Faith*, *Parenting by Prayer*, and *Made for Friendship*. She and her husband, Greg, have lived in Alaska, Washington D.C., and California. They now live in Wisconsin, where they are raising their three children.

**Andrea Delwiche** lives in Wisconsin with her husband, three kids, dog, cat, and a goldfish pond full of fish. She enjoys reading, knitting, and road-tripping with her family. Although a lifelong believer, she began to come into a deeper understanding of what it means to follow Christ far into adulthood (always a beginner on that journey!). Andrea has facilitated a Christian discussion group for women at her church for many years.

**Pastor Jon Enter** served as a pastor in West Palm Beach, Florida, for ten years. He is now a campus pastor and instructor at St. Croix Lutheran Academy in St. Paul, Minnesota. Jon also serves as a regular speaker on Grace Talks video devotions and a contributing writer to the ministry. He once led a tour at his college, and the Lord had him meet his future wife, Debbi. They are now drowning in pink and glitter with their four daughters: Violet, Lydia, Eden, and Maggie.

**Pastor Daron Lindemann** is pastor at a new mission start in Pflugerville, Texas. Previously, he served in downtown Milwaukee and in Irmo, South Carolina. Daron has authored articles or series for *Forward in Christ* magazine, *Preach the Word*, and his own weekly Grace MEMO devotions. He lives in Texas with his wife, Cara, and has two adult sons.

**Pastor David Scharf** served as a pastor in Greenville, Wisconsin, and now serves as a professor of theology at Martin Luther College in Minnesota. He has presented at numerous leadership, outreach, and missionary conferences across the country. He is a contributing writer for Time of Grace and a speaker for Grace Talks video devotions. Dave and his wife have six children.

**Pastor Clark Schultz** loves Jesus; his wife, Kristin, and their three boys; the Green Bay Packers; Milwaukee Brewers; Wisconsin Badgers; and—of course—Batman. His ministry stops are all in Wisconsin and include a vicar year in Green Bay, tutoring and recruiting for Christian ministry at a high school in Watertown, teacher/coach at a Christian high school in Lake Mills, and a pastor in Cedar Grove. He currently serves as a pastor in West Bend.

Pastor Clark's favorite quote is, "Find something you love to do and you will never work a day in your life."

**Christine Wentzel**, a native of Milwaukee, lives in Norfolk, Virginia, with her husband, James, and their fur-child, Piper. After two lost decades as a prodigal, Christine gratefully worships and serves her Salvation Winner at Resurrection in Chesapeake, Virginia. There she discovered latent talents to put to use for the Lord. In 2009 she began to write and create graphic design for an online Christian women's ministry, A Word for Women, and now also joyfully serves as a coadministrator for this ministry. www.awordforwomen.com

## About Time of Grace

Time of Grace is an independent, donor-funded ministry that connects people to God's grace—his love, glory, and power—so they realize the temporary things of life don't satisfy. What brings satisfaction is knowing that because Jesus lived, died, and rose for all of us, we have access to the eternal God—right now and forever.

To discover more, please visit timeofgrace.org or call 800.661.3311.

## Help share God's message of grace!

Every gift you give helps Time of Grace reach people around the world with the good news of Jesus. Your generosity and prayer support take the gospel of grace to others through our ministry outreach and help them experience satisfied lives as they see God all around them.

Give today at timeofgrace.org/give or by calling 800.661.3311.

Thank you!

**TIME OF GRACE**